Too Young to be This Old

A Mature Anthology

Sheryl Letzgus McGinnis

Topaz Publishing

READING ENTERTAINMENT
FOR THE ENTIRE FAMILY

Editor: Kase J. Reed

Line Editor: Chynna Laird, Topaz Publishing

ISBN: TPEB000000032

ISBN-13: 978-0615930275 Topaz Publishing
ISBN-10: 0615930271

Topaz Publishing, LLC

USA

www.topazpublishingllc.com

Topaz Publishing, LLC

Thank you for buying a product of Topaz Publishing

Quality Reading for the Entire Family

TOO YOUNG TO BE THIS OLD

Mature Anthology

A PRESCRIPTION FOR LOVE

Susan is an intelligent single woman who falls in love with a younger man...again. Hadn't she learned anything from her previous failed relationship?

THE CLASS REUNION

Fifty years ago, Ginger's heart was torn to shreds by a high school crush. Now, she has the opportunity to face the man who left her scrambling for a prom date. One day they were madly in love, then the next day, Sonny skipped town with a spoiled cheerleader.

I'M TOO YOUNG TO BE THIS OLD

Fiona is married, but feels she's too old for anything. To help her deal with her depression, her best friend enters her in a Dolly Parton look-alike contest.

A TORCH FOR DANIEL

Monica will never forget the love of her life. Although she moved on, her heart was still firmly attached to Daniel. Funeral services for his brother-in-law bring the couple face to face once again. Does Daniel still care?

DEDICATION

This book is lovingly dedicated to lovers everywhere, to those who have loved and lost, and to those who are fortunate to still have a special love in their lives. My husband, Jack, is my great love. He inspires me and he loves me. He owns my heart.

CONTENTS

Too Young to be This Old

A Mature Anthology

Have you ever looked at your reflection and a crinkled stranger stared back? Perhaps someone with hooded eyes and sinking jowls returned your gaze?

In this collection of short stories you will rediscover self-worth, gain encouragement, and uncover true friendship. Most of all, you will experience love and acceptance. Your future is bright, so face it with a smile. Learn the true value of being a mature woman—and find peace with yourself.

Inspirational, Mature Anthology

A PRESCRIPTION FOR LOVE

CHAPTER ONE

*A*fter removing her glasses, Susan peered through the vinyl blinds above her brocade sofa. Though it was early in the evening, she realized that a foot of snow had already fallen. The winter storm would make driving difficult, and surely, Andy would be late for dinner. Despite the bad weather, she still loved Raleigh, North Carolina.

Suddenly, her cell vibrated inside the pocket of her slacks. She retrieved it, then noticed Andy's name. After touching the screen, she placed the phone to her ear. "Hi Andy. What's wrong?"

"I'm gonna be late, Suze—another half-hour or so. This traffic's a bear. I'll be there, I promise. See ya in a little bit."

"That's odd," she remarked, while ending her call. *"Andy always says 'I love you' when he hangs up. It must be the stress of driving in such bad conditions."*

Fortunately for her, Susan had a few extra minutes to change from her business attire, and into something comfortable and sexy. She chose one of Andy's favorites—a vivid, pink, full-length sheath dress, paired with gold shoes. For their first Christmas together, Andy had given her a simple pair of expensive gold and diamond earrings. They would add an elegant touch to her attire.

The next fifteen minutes passed slowly. Susan busied herself by placing plates, utensils, and glasses on the coffee table. It was their custom to eat in the den, and then make love on the sofa in front of the television. Though their ritual had become routine, Andy wasn't typical of any males Susan had known. He was much younger—a pleaser, and seemed to enjoy making her happy. This loving trait, she relished.

For several weeks, Susan pondered why their relationship hadn't progressed beyond the physical. He was forty-one, and she was fifty-three. Was their age difference finally becoming a problem? She walked to the stove, picked up a potholder, then raised the lid on her casserole dish. The spicy aroma of her shrimp puttanesca enveloped her senses and she smiled. Inside the refrigerator, a decorative salad chilled; ready to be devoured by the couple. On the table, a lovely blueberry port was the perfect complement for the chocolate rum cheesecake she'd prepared the day before. Everything was almost ready, so where was Andy?

The doorbell rang and interrupted her thoughts. Susan closed the lid, tossed the potholder aside, then untied her apron. After flinging her blonde tresses over her shoulders, she pressed her lips together, then rushed toward the living room. Three years into the relationship and her anticipation was still amazing. She took a breath, then opened the door. "Andy. I'm glad you're here. With that awful weather, I was beginning to worry." She hugged and kissed him, noting a subtle lack of interest in his response. "Take off that wet coat, Sweetheart. Dinner will be another ten minutes. I'll open the Shiraz for now. "

Andy hung up his overcoat. He cleared his throat and turned to face Susan. An ashen smile crossed his face as he walked toward the couch. Obviously, he was nervous and ill at ease. "Suze, can we sit down?" He took a seat on one end of the couch and Susan followed, sitting opposite him. "I'm sorry," he said, as he stroked his forehead. "There's no easy way to start, but we need to talk. I didn't want to say this on the phone."

'*We need to talk*,' four words that portend an imminent heartbreak, instantly transformed a pleasant evening into a nightmare. Aware of the inevitable, Susan held her breath. "Okay."

Andy shifted in his seat, and lowered his dark brown eyes. After clasping his hands together, he gazed at her. "I love you, Suze. I really do, but—but I don't know how to put this into words."

Susan tapped her forefinger against her cheek, and stared at him. "Why don't you just say the first thing that comes to mind, Andy? Right off the top of your head. Then we can take it from there."

He elevated his gaze. "I love you."

"Yes," Susan murmured. "You've already said that. Say the second thing on your mind, then? Otherwise, we'll be here all night, stuck on one sentence. Just take a deep, slow breath and say it." She brightened her tone. "Or maybe you'd like me to say it for you. You love me, but you love someone else more— someone younger. Is that it?"

"No, that's not it at all. I don't want to sound like a broken record. It's true. I do love you, just not like before." Apparently crestfallen, Andy sighed. "It just seems the passion has gone out of our relationship. Not the physical passion. That's still there. You've always excited me, Suze. You still do, but I don't think we have the same emotional attachment anymore. I'm pretty sure you feel the same way." He frowned. "I sense it. Please say it isn't just me."

Susan hesitated, then plunged forward with the conversation. "I haven't wanted to admit it, but I think you're right. I agree, and it isn't a physical rut. We've never had a problem in that department." She lowered her eyes and continued. "I love you, too, Andy. Although, if we're honest with each other, we'd have to admit we're not *in* love. Is that what you were trying to say?"

"Yeah." He scratched his head. "I guess it is, and I'm so sorry about it. You're a beautiful, wonderful woman and…"

"Please. Don't bother," she interrupted. "You're a handsome, young, and wonderful man, but that isn't enough to sustain a serious relationship. I think we both deserve that. Don't get me wrong. I may sound philosophical about this, but it still hurts. I didn't expect to have this conversation tonight. You took the wind out of my sails. It'll take some time to digest this. Somehow, I suppose we'll manage to work together. Or do you have other plans?"

Andy's cheeks flushed. "As you know, my contract with the Cade Medical Clinic is up in two weeks. I'm sure you've been curious as to why I haven't renewed it." He hung his head and twiddled his thumbs. "It was a tough decision. I've accepted a position with a large medical group in Baltimore."

* * * * *

For over an hour they talked, not eating or drinking. Suze's dinner be darned. She'd lost her appetite, and obviously so had Andy. "You're an outstanding cook, Susan. I'm sorry the meal will go to waste. I just don't think I can hold anything down right now. I wouldn't want to make the situation worse by expelling the contents of my stomach on you." Andy's noticeable attempt at easing the situation had fallen flat.

"There's really nothing more to be said, is there? Better to end this here and now."

"Susan, I truly am sorry. I don't want to hurt you, but…"

"It's okay, Andy." She smoothed her dress. "Just go. We'll get through these next two weeks as friends. Enjoy your new life in Maryland. I wish you well."

Andy drew himself to his full 5'10 stature. His shaggy brown hair glistened as he ran his fingers through his mane. "Thanks, Suze. I—I guess I'll be going now."

Susan watched Andy walk out the door, and out of her life. "Drive carefully," she called, as she secured the door. Deep within, she realized her heart would mend. It had before. Where was her common sense when she fell in love with a younger man? She strolled to the table, then shrugged as she picked up the chilled bottle of wine. *"Well, no use letting good wine, and a good dessert go to waste."*

CHAPTER TWO

The weekly staff meetings had been less tedious the past two months since the board hired two new doctors, Dr. Sasha Benton and Dr. Blake Morrison. Although the staff missed Andy, the clinic was doing well with the addition of the new physicians.

Dr. Benton, a recent graduate of Emory University in Atlanta, had excellent credentials. The young woman was enthusiastic, and eager to begin her career as an internist at Cade Medical Clinic.

Pretty, and tall enough to be a supermodel, Sasha had sufficient intelligence to get whatever she wanted. Susan realized this fact during their first two interviews. Foremost, Susan was professional enough to understand what the clinic needed in their new physicians, and Sasha had the necessary qualifications. Therefore, Susan made sure nothing upset the clinic's apple cart.

With all the physicians, nurses, and ancillary staff meshing, Cade Medical ran like a well-oiled machine. Outspoken and opinionated, Dr. Benton clashed with Susan on more than one occasion, which caused the meetings to be quite heated at times. *"Even the best families quibble,"* Susan reasoned. As long as Sasha didn't step over professional lines, she was willing to cut her some slack.

On the other hand, Dr. Morrison was an affable, highly skilled cardiologist, who had received training at one of the top four hospitals in the United States, the Cleveland Clinic, in Cleveland, Ohio.

Dr. Blake Morrison was young and uncommonly handsome. He stood 6'1, and wore his long blonde hair in a stylish cut. With his dazzling smile, he could have had a career as a movie star. As a testament to his kind and compassionate nature, even the males in the group liked and respected him.

Along with the other females on staff, Susan found herself captivated by his polished charm. Yet, she wouldn't allow herself to fall for another younger man. She'd been burned once, and refused to revisit that horrible experience.

CHAPTER THREE

The annual physicians' retreat was imminent. Attentive as she was, Susan had booked a resort in Gatlinburg, Tennessee. Her hands were full as she arranged everything. Though she planned four days of intense business meetings, she left the evenings free so the staff could relax.

During the conclusion of the first day, Susan and the doctors found themselves eager to unwind. They gathered in the main dining room of the lodge to enjoy an evening of music, good food, and lively companionship. Susan stood in a small group, chatting with co-workers. From across the room, she watched Blake while he played-out his social role. Finally, their eyes met. He smiled flirtatiously, as he'd done since she'd hired him. Not wanting to become involved with another physician, especially one so much younger, she always rebuffed his advances.

Susan lowered her glasses, smiled, and then turned her attention to the people in her circle. Soon, she felt a presence behind her, followed by a firm hand on her waist. Stunned, she turned in response.

"Susan." Dr. Morrison grinned slyly. "How are you?" Though Blake maintained his grip on Susan's waist, he greeted each person in the group.

Dr. Lassiter reached for his hand. "Blake. Glad you've joined us. It was fortunate that you and Dr. Benton joined us at Cade Medical."

"You've both been a great addition to our organization," Dr. Bethune commented with a warm smile.

Blake removed his hand from Susan's waist and shook hands with Dr. Lassiter, and then Dr. Bethune, thanking them for their congeniality. He turned toward Susan, flashing a sexy smile. "Getting hired by Cade Medical was a great day for me, too. I've enjoyed working with everyone, especially your great administrator."

Blake moved closer to Susan. Noting the obvious, she flinched as their bodies touched. "*This is ridiculous*," she thought. "*He's being very friendly. Too friendly, in fact.*"

Dr. Lassiter extended his hand. "Susan. Dance with me." He turned to Blake. "Please excuse us, but Susan and I love this song." They walked onto the shimmering dance floor and danced to an oldie but goodie. "You're a great dancer, Susan. Don't tell my wife I said that," he teased. "I don't know which I prefer best, dancing with you, or watching you shake your booty." Luke gave a hearty laugh. Clearly, he was delighted by his own humorous remark.

Susan had been the CEO of Cade Medical, for over three years. During that time she learned that Luke was all bluff. He loved his wife, and would never hurt her. He and Susan were good friends, and nothing more. Luke was her strongest ally when she needed backup with an unruly physician.

Luke placed his hand on Susan's waist and pulled her close. "I noticed how Blake invaded your personal space this evening. I think he's sweet on you."

Susan leaned back and gazed into his slightly aging eyes. "Now there's an old-timey expression. Are you sure you're forty-five and not sixty-five?"

"Whatever. I still say he's sweet on you. Would you rather I said, he wants to jump your bones?" Dr. Lassiter glanced at her. "It's more than that. Yep, he's definitely sweet on you."

"Oh please. He's forty-three years old and — and I'm not." She laughed with a wisp of regret in her voice.

"Yeah, but you're hot stuff." Luke twirled her around, and seemed to admire the view.

"Well, he *is* good looking. I'll give you that. And, in another five years, he'll be really handsome. For now, he's got a baby face."

"Come on. You wouldn't do him? Really?"

With a giggle, Susan admitted, "Funny, but I don't recall saying *that*." Her words surprised her. "But seriously, I wouldn't. I just had one affair with a physician end badly, so I've sworn off doctors. It isn't good business anyway. Andy and I were already dating when I became the CEO of Cade. Nobody should have a problem with that."

"I know. You're right, too." He flashed a broad smile. "It's not wise to date within the company, especially physicians. We tend to have a pretty high opinion of ourselves. You may have noticed," he admitted with a wink.

The song ended, and they walked back toward their fellow physicians. Susan felt a twinge of discontent when she noticed that Blake was no longer among them. While feigning interest in the dance floor she scanned the room for her lost companion. Disappointment turned to jealousy when Susan discovered Blake near the doors leading to the deck. There, he engaged in what appeared to be earnest conversation with Sasha Benton. *"Where did that come from?"* she mused. Susan wasn't the jealous type, and she had no designs on a forty-three-year-old. Or did she? Vexed, she struggled to concentrate on the conversation. "I'm sorry. Yes, you're right. Absolutely." She had no idea what Dr. Montgomery was right about, but she hoped it wouldn't come back to bite her.

Within minutes, Blake held Sasha in his arms, dancing to one of Susan's favorites.

"Why is this bothering me so much? He means nothing to me. He's ten years younger than I am. Get a grip, Susan," she commanded herself. *"He definitely was flirting with me though."*

"Susan? Suze? Hello?" Dr. Montgomery spoke again. "I'd give much more than a penny for your thoughts. I see you standing here, but your mind's a million miles away. Everything okay?"

"I'm sorry, Joe," Susan answered with a big smile. "I was thinking about our meetings tomorrow. I have so much to do. I shouldn't waste my time like this."

Susan begged off, and apologized for retiring early. She'd see them in the morning, bright and early, for a full day of discussions about the future of Cade Medical Clinic.

As Susan exited the main dining room, she decided to catch a breath of fresh air before turning in for the night. She walked onto the large deck that surrounded the lodge. Her thoughts turned to Andy. She wondered about his new life in Maryland. *"Do I really miss him, or is it just loneliness? I'll admit I do miss our physical relationship."*

"Hey, Susan. Enjoying this beautiful night?" came a male's voice from the darkness. It was Blake's sensual tone. Not only Blake, but Sasha, too. They walked toward her with Sasha's arm looped through his. Apparently, Sasha didn't feel the need to say anything. She gave Susan a furtive smile, and then pulled Blake a little closer. When they stopped walking, Sasha leaned near, and kissed Blake on the cheek.

"Oh. Hey guys," Susan answered with a stammer. "Yes, it's been a wonderful night, but I've got some papers to go over before our meeting tomorrow morning. I'm going to turn in early. Goodnight. Enjoy the rest of your evening."

Sasha raised a brow. "Oh, I'm sure we *will*." She switched her gaze from Blake to Susan, then gave her an 'I've-got-him-and-you-don't smile. "It's going to be a long, beautiful night, isn't it, Blake?"

Susan noticed an odd look on Blake's face as he turned to walk away, but she wasn't sure what it meant. *"The heck with you, Sasha. I wonder what you'd think if you knew Blake had a habit of flirting with me. Darn it. Why am I letting this bother me? They can have each other for all I care."* As she pondered the curious expression on Blake's face, she walked along the deck, headed toward her room.

* * * * *

After Susan entered her room, she locked the door behind her. She dropped her purse on the table, removed her heels, and walked barefooted into the bathroom. On her journey, she pulled a bottle of wine from the mini refrigerator.

15

Inside the bathroom, Susan placed the bottle aside, then turned on the faucet to the sunken tub. The sounds of gurgling water echoed off the tiled walls. *"A soothing bubble bath will erase all those bad memories."* Susan poured herself a glass of chardonnay. Goblet in hand, she placed it on the vanity. Next, she lit the fragrant complementary candles the hotel provided. *"Mmm, pear blossoms. How relaxing."* With everything prepared, she placed her hair into a clip, removed her clothes, and then dropped them to the floor. Because the next day would be stressful, she decided to take advantage of this respite.

Once the tub was full, Susan dipped her toe into the warm water. The temperature was perfect, so she eased into the tub. Immediately, her thoughts drifted back to Blake. He was handsome and sexy, and his flirtations flattered her. After she retrieved the wine, she sipped the nectar. The brew relaxed her, and allowed repressed desire for Blake to surface. *"I've got to be honest with myself. I have more than admiration for Blake. I want him."* There, she'd admitted it. All thoughts of Andy were erased; she longed to have Blake's masculine arms wrapped around her.

A soft rap on the door interrupted her reverie and annoyed her. She'd have to put on her robe, and contend with whatever problem some pesky doctor might have. *"Please. Not now. Just let me relax and enjoy my thoughts. Tomorrow's going to be a long day, and I need some 'me' time right now."*

Susan considered ignoring the intrusion of her privacy. If she didn't attend to the situation, the pest would probably persist. "Just a second," she yelled, rising from her delightful bath. She slipped into her terry robe, and then made her way to the door.

With one eye pressed against the peephole, Suze was astonished to see Blake. The absence of Sasha brought her a surge of relief.

Embarrassed by her appearance, she pulled the robe around her, then opened the door. "Come in, Blake. This is a surprise — to say the least. I was just about to take a bath when I heard you knock. If you'll give me a minute, I'll put my clothes back on and…"

Blake lowered his eyes to the water dripping down Susan's legs. He gazed into her eyes, walked closer, and smirked. "That's the opposite effect I had hoped for."

"Very funny." She removed the clip from her hair and lowered it about her shoulders. "What can I do for you, anyway? Why are you here? Wait. Before you tell me, I really do have to put my clothes on. I'm a little uncomfortable talking to you while wearing my robe."

"I understand. It's not my intention to embarrass you. May I have a glass of that wine while you're changing?"

"Of course, help yourself. Have a seat. There's an extra glass on the counter. I won't be long."

Within a minute, Susan returned, clothed in a pair of sexy jeans and a soft cashmere sweater that hugged her curves. "There, I feel better now. So, where's Sasha? What happened to her?"

As he reclined on the love seat, a chuckle rumbled in Blake's chest. "Don't know. Don't care." With a devilish grin, he added, "Great sweater."

"Thank you," she replied, and blushed. "So, Sasha blew you off? I got the impression she really wanted you. What happened?"

"Oh, she wanted me all right. Although, I believe her main goal was to keep us apart. I probably shouldn't say this, but she said some pretty catty things about you."

"Well, I was right then. I caught those vibes from her, not to mention the death rays she shot me. She has nothing to worry about. There's nothing going on between us…"

"Not just yet, there isn't." Blake laughed as he tipped his glass to Susan.

With narrowed eyes, Susan parted her lips. "Behave yourself, doctor."

"Come on, you must know I'm attracted to you — very attracted to you. Since I've joined the staff at Cade, I've taken every opportunity to flirt with you. I hoped you'd reciprocate.

Tonight, when I stood next to you, I thought I'd explode."

"Blake." Susan folded her arms. "I'm ten years older than you. That means when I was twenty-three, you were thirteen. When I was thirteen, you were three. Think about it."

"Yes, I've heard that argument before. But contrariwise, you gorgeous creature, that means when you're eighty-three, I'll be seventy-three. Not such a difference, right?" He laughed, as he beckoned her to sit beside him on the sofa.

Susan retrieved her glass of wine from the bathroom, and then sat next to Blake. His thigh brushed hers; she bit her lip, every part of her body aflame. She closed her eyes to compose herself. When she opened them, she explained, "But this is now, Blake. I'm fifty-three and you're forty-three."

"Almost forty-four," Blake contradicted. "So that makes the age difference only about nine years now. We're getting closer together."

"By a matter of months? You call that close? Good thing you aren't a math teacher," Susan laughed. "People would call you my *Boy Toy*."

* * * * *

They spent the next half hour drinking wine, and getting to know each other. It amazed Susan how much they had in common, in spite of their age difference. Blake was more like a contemporary than her junior. When she looked at him, she saw a pleasant, decent man looking back. Another bottle of wine found them loosening up even more, and they knew where this was headed.

Placing his glass on the coffee table, Blake slid closer, then cupped her face with his hand.

"Do you think this is wise, I mean…"

"Sh." Blake pulled Susan closer, and gently kissed her brow. Then, he kissed the tip of her nose, followed by her cheeks.

She tingled as his lips pressed hard against hers. His firm embrace thrilled her. "We shouldn't be doing this," Susan whispered, pushing him aside.

"But we *are* doing this. Admit it. It feels right. I think you want me as much as I want you. Well, maybe not as much as *I* want *you*, but just give it time. You'll find the age difference will just disappear. It really doesn't matter. I've wanted you since the first interview."

"Blake, you don't understand."

"I understand this, Susan. 'What's sauce for the goose is sauce for the gander'. Although in this case, I suppose we should technically say, 'what's sauce for the gander is sauce for the goose'. Why should men be the only ones allowed to date younger people? It's time society moved past that outmoded notion, don't you think? Disdaining women who date younger men is nothing more than ageism, perpetrated by women who can't get a younger man."

"But, wouldn't that make me a cougar?" Susan chuckled. "You do make good points though."

Blake put his arm around Susan, and leaned her against the sofa. Again, he kissed her, and she returned his ardor with equal passion. In his arms, Susan realized she'd never experienced that type of passion with Andy.

She reveled in the sensations as Blake covered her with kisses. He may have been a younger man, but he had a world of experience in the art of love. A perfect fit physically, the couple spent the night in total bliss. Susan gave her all, as did Blake.

"Thank you for not dismissing me out of hand," Blake murmured. "I told you we're right for each other."

Susan purred in his ear, "You would have made a great salesman, Blake. You're a man of many talents."

"As are you, a woman of extraordinary talents. I think I've met my match." Blake stood, grasped Susan's hand, and helped her to her feet. "I believe you were drawing a hot bath before I interrupted you. You wanna add some hot water and go soak for a while? There's still Chardonnay left."

CHAPTER FOUR

The next morning found Susan and the other physicians around the conference table. Coffee, orange juice, fresh fruit, yogurt, and baskets of bagels had been provided. There were also various flavors of cream cheese.

A lengthy discussion about Cade Medical Clinic's future took place by the panel. They broke for lunch from 1:00 to 2:00 p.m. When they returned, the meeting would continue until the evening, which signaled the end of day two.

Sasha remained unusually quiet during the debates, not offering much input. When the meeting adjourned, Susan remained to clean up and stack papers. Eager to get started with their evening activities, everyone left the conference room in a hurry. Sasha sidled to Blake, and whispered something in his ear.

Blake's mouth fell open. He responded with a look of disgust while Sasha's face turned crimson. She glanced over her shoulder at Susan, then turned on her heels, and stormed out.

Blake lingered in the room, and curiosity got the better of Susan. "Blake, what was that all about? I feel somehow she blames me for something."

He guided Susan to the door and opened it. "Let's go back to my room before dinner, okay? We can talk along the way." The couple strolled along the carpeted floor toward Blake's suite. "I'm telling you, Susan. Sasha may be a brilliant physician, but she's a she-devil. According to her, she wanted to go back to my room, and give me the best time I've ever had. I declined. She doesn't know it, but I've already had the best time ever." Blake smiled and stroked Susan's back. "I'm quite serious about that, too. You're all the woman I need."

"Well, I'm glad you didn't say anything to her. You turned down a woman who doesn't take *no* for an answer, that's enough humiliation. I do have a question about last night though."

"Hmmm, do I want to hear this question? Does it have anything to do with my performance? Don't answer if it does."

"Last night your performance was quite extraordinary. This morning, too, as you well know," Susan mumbled, as she squeezed Blake's hand. "This is about last night; when I saw you and Sasha on the deck. While you were leaving, you had a strange look on your face. I didn't quite know what to make of it."

"Did it look like this?" Blake recreated his expression from the previous night—the look of a man who wanted to be rescued. "I didn't want to be with her. She hijacked me onto the dance floor. Then, with my arm in a vise, she led me onto the deck. All I could think about was you, and how much I wanted to be with you."

"I don't know if you're sincere, or just full of it. Whatever it is, you sure know how to make a girl feel special."

The couple continued down the hallway. Suddenly, Blake stopped at room 406. "This is my room." A seductive glint brightened his eyes. Let's go inside, and I'll show you how special you are."

Susan gazed at the door and sighed. "Sasha doesn't go down without a fight, does she? I mean, she will try again this evening. If she wasn't such a good doctor, I'd fire her and make her spin her web in somebody else's clinic. Having designs on you isn't a good cause for her dismissal, at least, not legally."

"Let's not waste another breath with this discussion." Blake unlocked the door, ushered Susan inside, then followed, closing the door behind them. He removed his jacket and threw it on the chair. Turning his attention to Susan, he kissed her while he unbuttoned her blouse. In his haste, he lost his balance, tripped over his shoes and stumbled. The two fell into the nightstand, sending the lamp toppling to the floor. Giggling, they hit the edge of the bed and then tumbled onto the carpet.

"This will be something to tell our grandchildren." Blake laughed as he rolled onto his back, pulling Susan on top of him. "Kiss me, you beautiful woman."

They made love right there. The passion was every bit as exquisite as their earlier encounters.

* * * * *

The next two days and nights were repeats of the same. However, Susan knew she couldn't continue the relationship. Since Blake's comment about grandchildren, she'd been uneasy. Because of her age, she had given up any hopes of children. Blake tried to reassure her that many women have children after fifty. While they were in Gatlinburg, she let it go. Yet, she realized once they returned to Raleigh, the issue would need to be revisited and finalized.

CHAPTER FIVE

It had been two months since Susan called off the relationship with Blake. *"What relationship,"* she asked herself. It had been only four passion-filled days, a fling. Nothing more.

Blake used his rather persuasive charms to convince her otherwise, but Susan was adamant; she was not the woman for him. She insisted he needed a childbearing woman more his age — a woman with fresher eggs.

Staff meetings proved difficult for the two of them as the air was thick with tension. Only Dr. Lassiter was aware of their Gatlinburg affair, or at least that's what Susan hoped. It was difficult to determine if Sasha knew they had an assignation, or just surmised it. If any of the others knew, they were polite enough, and professional enough, not to say anything. And Blake had remained discreet.

Susan longed for his kisses and his gentle touch, coupled with his incredible passion. She missed their easy conversations and the laughter they shared over the silliest things. Although, she longed for everything about him, she didn't want to hold him back. He loved children, and wanted them, as did she. The ultimate reason for her actions, however, stemmed from abandonment issues. She refused to be rejected by a younger man.

Truthfully, it would have been nice to have children of her own. Her brother, John's, two daughters were a delight to her. She loved shopping and doing girly things with them. At seven and eight years of age, they were a lot of fun and clearly loved their Aunt Susan. *"They'll just have to do,"* Susan told herself. *"I love them as if they were my own, and I'm fortunate to have them in my life."*

* * * * *

Much to Susan's liking, the weather was getting warmer. However, no one seemed to like an unseasonably warm Christmas. Saturday morning was her favorite time of the day. As she poured her second cup of coffee, her cell rang. She reached on the counter, and saw Andy's name on the screen. "Hello?"

"Susan?"

She smiled. "Andy! Hello."

"Hi, Susan. I hope I'm not bothering you. I just got back in town. Thought I'd take a chance and call you. It would've been best to call you from Maryland, but I hoped the passage of time would smooth things."

With phone in hand, Susan walked into the living room and paced before the sofa. "There's nothing to smooth, Andy. It's good to hear from you. If I were a gambling woman, I'd bet your arms are laden with gifts for your nieces and nephews. Am I right?"

"Are you ever wrong, Suze? You know me better than I know myself. I feel sorry for kids on Christmas morning when they find Santa didn't bring them anything. All the toys are at my sister's house." Andy chortled.

"You do spoil them. They'd be glad to see you, even without toys."

"Well, I was wondering if you'd be glad to see me. I know the annual Cade Christmas party is next Saturday, and I hope to attend. Would that be okay with you?"

Susan stopped pacing and sat down on her sofa. "It's not only okay, but if you don't have a date, you can be my plus one. I'm going stag. Well, Dr. Brandon is going with me, but she's not a date." Susan smirked.

"Sounds great. Shall I pick you up, or meet you there?"

"Actually, I'd like you to pick me up. Pick both of us up. That way Karla and I can have more champagne than we should, and we won't have to worry about driving home, trying to catch a cab, or begging somebody to take pity on our poor drunken souls."

"Okay, I'm sold," Andy agreed. "I'll pick you and Karla up, and then take you home when it's over. That is, if you don't get a better offer."

"Thanks, Andy. I doubt there will be any better offers. It'll be nice to see you again. We shouldn't be enemies, especially since we cared so much for each other."

"Ah, Saint Susan. You always were too good for me. I agree we should never be enemies. I've never thought of you as such, and I'm glad you don't think of me that way. I'll always consider you my friend. Perhaps, that's all we should have ever been."

"You may be right, but we did have some good times in the beginning. I choose to remember those times."

"So do I. Well, we can talk about them Saturday. Pick you up at eight o'clock, right?"

"Sure. See you then." She sighed. "And, Andy? Thanks."

CHAPTER SIX

"Wow! And double wow!" Andy exclaimed as Susan opened her front door. Karla stood grinning beside her.

"Come inside, handsome. It's chilly out." Susan laughed, and Andy hurried inside.

Andy gave her a timid kiss on the cheek, and then turned his attention to Karla, kissing her, too. "You both look sensational. I'd like to have half the money you each spent on those dresses."

"I don't know what you're talking about. These platform pumps complement my little designer dress. Don't you think? As you can see, Karla is wearing a designer's original. Just a little something we threw together at the last minute." Susan shoved Karla playfully and she chuckled.

"Oh, I'm sorry," Andy teased. "I didn't mean to insult you ladies. How dare I imply that you're spending a small fortune on your outfits? I should say a freaking *large* fortune."

Susan beamed. "That's funny coming from Mr. Savile Row, but you've got that right. Between the two of us, Karla and I donate a small fortune to our charities. Once in a great while, it feels good to splurge on ourselves. Society will forgive us an occasional indulgence."

"Yeah," Karla chimed in, "and then we feel so guilty. We'll double our contributions. It's a win-win situation."

"Well," Andy moved his eyes over the shapely pair, "whatever you spent is certainly worth it. You ladies are dazzling. I'll be the most envied man at the party tonight. Shall we go? Your chariot awaits. At least, what passes for a chariot from the rental agency."

They opened the door, looking past the only vehicle parked outsidea white stretch limo.

"Is that limo yours?" Susan exclaimed. "Andy? You hired a limo? Are you serious?"

"Follow me," he said, placing his palm in the bare small of Susan's back. "And yes, I'm absolutely serious. Why should you two have all the fun tonight? We can all drink way more champagne than we should. And who knows; we might even fool around a little."

Susan draped her cape around her neck, then gazed at Karla. They burst into laughter. It was going to be an interesting Christmas party.

* * * * *

As they stepped into the ballroom of the Renaissance Raleigh at North Hills, all eyes focused on the threesome. The festive décor created a jovial atmosphere. Everyone seemed to be in a celebratory mood, and Susan felt quite special in her expensive haute couture. *"Special. Blake thought I was special."*

Quite dapper in his tux, Dr. Montgomery walked over to the threesome and asked Karla to dance. As he swirled her around the dance floor, Susan pondered, *"They make a handsome couple."*

While the orchestra played *White Christmas*, Andy placed his hand on Susan's back, then led her onto the dance floor. She knew the Christmas songs wouldn't go on all night. The band would eventually perform rock and roll, interspersed with slow music. Couples could snuggle as they danced.

Andy's arms felt good and Susan couldn't deny it. But unfortunately, her thoughts were with Blake. *"Why did I break off the relationship with Blake?"* she mused. *"Why? Why? Because of the age difference? Because he wanted a child? Or was it because of a previous, humiliating, relationship failure?"*

Rationally, Susan knew she wasn't old. *"For heaven's sake, I'm only fifty-three,"* she reminded herself. *"That's still young. Still, it's older than Blake. There is no avoiding it."* She was ten years older, or a little over nine years according to his calculations.

"Where is Blake," she wondered, scanning the room. He'd mentioned to Dr. Ostrosky at the staff meeting that he was coming to the annual Christmas party. Though he didn't tell

her personally, he made sure she overheard his plans.

Blake no longer talked to her about anything other than business. Their red-hot fling had deteriorated into a platonic relationship, which Susan believed displeased him. Why did he have such difficulty accepting her position about their age difference?

Although Susan danced with Andy, in her heart Blake held her. Her fantasy came to a sudden halt when she spotted Blake talking with Sasha by the dance floor. *"Again?"* she thought, as she recalled the last time she saw them together. *"Humph, talk about déjà vu. Oh Blake. If only I hadn't been such an idiot. What's ten years? I mean, really. Why did I make such a big deal out of it? Ten little, no, make that about nine little years. That's it. How did I ever get to be CEO of a large company when I'm such a total moron?"*

While Blake danced with Sasha, his gaze followed Susan wherever she was. Though she didn't acknowledge his attention, she felt his eyes watching her every move. *"Are they a couple now?"* she wondered. *"If so, why is he smiling when I look his way?"*

When Sasha and Blake headed toward the exit, Susan's hopes faded. *"Where are they going?"* she questioned, as if she didn't know. Trying to develop a plan, Susan's mind raced.

While Susan contemplated her strategy, Blake and Sasha stopped near the exit to visit with Dr. Ostrosky and his nurse. After what seemed to be a pleasant conversation, Blake shook Dr. Ostrosky' s hand. It surprised Susan when Blake said his goodbyes to Dr. Ostrosky, his nurse and…Sasha? He turned to walk away from Sasha, but she grabbed his elbow, attempting to spin him around. Blake shrugged her off, and continued walking toward the door. While doctor and his nurse stared in wonder, Sasha stood red-faced.

Susan held her breath as Blake walked toward her. She wanted to run to him and throw her arms around him, but she refrained. What would he do? It would serve her right if he ignored her. *"He couldn't,"* she mused, *"or could he?"* She'd soon find out.

CHAPTER SEVEN

"Susan," Blake called, walking toward her. "Could we talk? Please? Not here. Would you take a walk with me, somewhere quiet?"

"Oh no, not the 'we need to talk' conversation." Susan's mind raced. *"This never ends well. Been there, done that."*

Before Susan could respond, Blake placed his arm around her waist and led her into an unoccupied banquet room.

Blake indicated that Susan sit on a beautiful floral settee, then he sat beside her, and took her hands. "Please, bear with me. I know you aren't interested in me romantically, but that doesn't mean I'm not...well, what I'm trying to say is..."

Before he could complete his statement, Susan interrupted. "I love you."

"You what?" Blake exclaimed, his eyes widened with surprise. "I'd better see a hearing specialist. I could swear you just said, you love me." Taking Susan in his arms, he caressed her lightly.

"I do love you," she whispered. "I've loved you since the first night we spent together in Gatlinburg."

Looking into Susan's eyes, Blake frowned. "If you love me, why did you turn me away? It can't be our age difference. I just can't buy that. You know that doesn't matter."

"I know that." She cast her gaze toward the floor. "If I were truthful, I'd tell you I'm afraid you'll leave me for a younger woman. It's that simple."

"Oh my." He shook his head. "I could never leave you for any reason. I'm in love with you, Susan. You'll just have to trust my love."

Through Susan's smile, tears of joy flooded her face. Using a cocktail napkin, she wiped her eyes. "I've been left for a younger woman before. Ten years ago, I was forty-three and he was…"

"Let me guess, twenty-three?"

"No, he was fifty-three! The old coot left me for a twenty-five-year old." Susan laughed. A mixture of sadness and regret laced her voice. "I was too old for him. Can you imagine that? I've carried the scars of that embarrassment for ten years. Only Luke knew about it, and now you."

Blake kissed Susan's hands. Then, he feathered hot kisses from the base of her neck to her chin. When their lips met, she greeted him with explosive passion. "I knew there had to be more to this than a silly little nine year age difference. You could have told me. There's nothing for you to be embarrassed about. This was all on him, not you. His loss, ten years ago, has given me the greatest Christmas present."

"I know. You're right. But, sometimes we carry a load of emotional baggage that no amount of rationalization can fix."

"Well, we're going to put this baby to rest. Maybe not right this instant, but it's something we'll work on together. I've never been happier." Blake wrapped his arms around her. As he stroked her back, he kissed her. "If you didn't look so sensational in that dress I'd rip it off you right now.

Susan felt her cheeks redden. "Even in my wildest imagination, I couldn't have envisioned this happening tonight. Oh, Blake, Blake…"

He lifted her chin, and kissed her lips tenderly. "I don't know about you, but I've suddenly got a voracious appetite. Shall we go back into the ballroom and partake of that delicious food, Madame?"

"Absolutely, I'm famished. I also need to let Andy and Karla know I won't be sharing the limo with them on the way home. I'm also hungry for answers. For instance, why were you with Sasha tonight? Why were you two talking to Dr. Ostrosky? Why did you leave Sasha with him?"

Blake chuckled. "You're certainly the little question box. One, Sasha cornered me as she always does whenever she gets the chance. She's not going to give up until we're married. I mean, until you and I are married, of course."

Shock and surprise overcame Susan. With an air of lighthearted humor, she asked, "Did you just propose to me, or lay out a plan to rid yourself of Sasha?"

"Hold that thought. Let me answer your other questions. First, I mean second, Sasha wanted to talk to Dr. Ostrosky about covering for her next week, so I walked with her. I figured it would be easier to extricate myself from her clutches if she had something else to focus on. Worked like a charm."

Susan bit her lip. "You're something else. Life with you would be very interesting."

He took her hands, and smiled. "*Will* be, Susan."

"Will be what?" Hearing his words, Susan leaned back unsure of his intentions.

"Well, Susan. You said life with me *would* be interesting. No, it *will* be interesting. And yes that was a proposal. It isn't how I would have planned it, but tonight was such a surprise. If you say no, I'll grovel and beg, but I won't give up. I love you, and I want to spend the rest of my life with you."

"I love you too. I didn't realize until tonight just how much. I want to grow old with you." Susan looked at Blake and grinned. "And I look forward to being an old lady married to a Boy Toy of seventy-three."

~The End~

THE CLASS REUNION

CHAPTER ONE

$\mathcal{D}$ressed in a comfortable warm-up suit, Ginger stood in the kitchen of her country home, talking to her best friend on the phone. "Sandy, guess who I just found on Facebook?" she giggled. "Actually, I didn't find him. He found me and asked to be my friend. You'll never guess, so I'll just tell you. Tony Devito. Remember him?"

"Tony. Our old classmate. Wow! That was 1963, fifty years ago. What a blast from the past. Of course, I remember him. Everybody liked him because he was so sweet. He may have been short, but he sure had a tall personality. If memory serves me correctly, he was voted *Best Dressed Guy* in our senior year. I remember how the Best Dressed Girl towered over him in the yearbook picture. Maureen Mc, somebody or other. Can't remember her last name now. Can you believe that? I just remember she was an only child, and spoiled rotten. Always had the latest fashions from pencil skirts, to the Black Watch plaid pinafores. Back then, we thought those things were so hot."

With her cell in one hand and a diet drink in the other, Ginger paced back and forth—her custom whenever she was on the phone. When trying to keep in shape the smallest bit of exercise counted, and pacing was her way to keep moving.

"Yep," Ginger reminisced. "I remember Maureen Mitchell. We were all jealous of her, especially after she became a cheerleader. Except me of course, because I was a cheerleader, too. We used to argue about which one of us cheered the best, but we all knew it was me. At least, that's how I remember it." Ginger laughed. "Speaking of Tony, we'll get to see him again. He contacted me to let me know our fifty-year high school reunion is coming up in six weeks. Can you believe that? Fifty years! Where has the time gone?"

"I don't know Ginge," Sandy replied pensively. "You had a wonderful job as a travel writer, and then you settled down with a great man. I sold real estate and had a wonderful daughter. My one regret is marrying her lying, cheating, womanizing father."

"He was a good father to Chloe, though, so I guess he wasn't all bad. Besides, we shouldn't speak ill of the dead. You did plenty of that while the rat was still alive. I'm just sayin'."

"You always make my day, sweetie." Sandy laughed. "I suppose we shouldn't complain."

Ginger tossed the soda can in the recycle bin, before leaning on the counter to stare out the window. Outside, an ominous storm was rolling in. The crash of thunder and a flash of lightning illuminated the kitchen, evoking bittersweet memories. She thought of the happy times she'd spent with Bill in that same kitchen. During storms, they enjoyed sipping coffee or drinking specially brewed teas. "I know. I've had so much, but what I wouldn't give to have Bill back. Sometimes, I still expect him to walk through the door, even though it's been ten years since he passed away. I miss him so much."

"Yes," Sandy hesitated, "it's awful. I lost Dan to other women long before he died. For some reason, he couldn't seem to settle down. We've learned to accept our fate, which has made us stronger. Otherwise, we never would've been able to adjust to our new lives. Hold on just a sec. Candace is on the other line. Let me tell her that I'll call her back."

While Ginger waited for Sandy to return to the phone, she plucked another can of diet soda from the fridge, then continued to pace. She set the soft drink on the counter, and then added a few jumping jacks to her routine until Sandy came back.

"You'll never believe it, Ginge, but Candice wanted to tell me about the class reunion, too. I wonder why we didn't know. Now, it seems everybody's talking about it. Maybe we waited a little too long to hop on board the technology train, huh?"

"Well, I'm glad we finally did. That gives us enough time to lose a few pounds." Gazing at her lightly protruding belly, Ginger laughed. She looked at Miss Kitty curled up on the window seat. *"Even my cat could lose a pound or two herself."*

Sandy's voice drew her attention. "We're both going, right?"

"Honey, wild horses couldn't keep me away from this event. I wonder what the old geezers look like today." No sooner had she spat out the words, Ginger nearly choked on her soda.

"I don't know how to break it to you girlfriend," Sandy joked, "but we're old geezers, too. This is our 50th reunion—and not our 25th"

"Well, you're right about that. We're in the geezer class now, I suppose. I don't think we look it. That's my story, and I'm sticking to it."

"We don't think old either. We're definitely young at heart, and we're fun people. So we'll go, have a good time, and renew old friendships. We can meet for lunch the next day to rehash the entire night."

Miss Kitty padded into the kitchen, and Ginger turned in response. "It's a done deal. Gotta go. Miss Kitty has gotten up. She's winding around my legs, and purring for her treat. Talk to you later."

While Ginger struggled to open the catnip, she bent down, lifted Miss Kitty, and cradled her in one arm while pouring the treats into the bowl. "You're lucky you're so adorable, girl, because you're one spoiled cat. And you're a bit large around the middle, too. We'll have to do something about that."

Ginger removed a few treats from the bowl, and poured them back into the container. Trying to retrieve her treats, Miss Kitty swiped at Ginger's hand. Her dissatisfaction with her owner's temerity was evident by her meows.

CHAPTER TWO

Ginger and Sandy spent hours each day discussing the upcoming reunion. Together, they shopped for just the right dress until each had found the perfect frock.

Inside the dressing room, Sandy admired her reflection in the mirror, careful to hold her chin up as she did so. "You know, we might be what some would call *old broads,* but I'll be darned if we can't still rock a sexy silk dress."

"Hello? I think the only thing we can rock today is a rocking chair, girl. If we're lucky, we can rock it without falling off. Yeah. That's what I'm sayin'. Without being too immodest, I do believe you're right. We don't look too bad for umm, women of a certain age."

"That's one heck of a euphemism, Ginge. I still say we can rock a sexy dress, no matter what age we are."

"As long as the dress sleeves are long enough to hide these darn bat wings. Gravity gets us in the most inconvenient places. Faces, eyelids, chins, necks, arms and, of course, our most prized possessions — the girls." Ginger cupped her generous breasts with both hands. She held them up and sighed. "The elevator doesn't go up to that floor anymore. It's just straight down, heading rapidly and inexorably to the knees. Even they sag. Think we can get a full body lift in time for the reunion?"

Bursting into laughter, they both held their breasts up and pranced around the changing room. Alternately, each pulled her facial skin back while tugging her eyelids. Much like they'd done when they were young girls, the friends collapsed in a heap of laughter on the chaise.

As Sandy stood, she wiped the tears from her cheeks, then eyed herself in the mirror. "You know what, Ginger?"

"No. What? Are you going to tell me about another area that sags? Oh right, how could I forget about my beautiful, bodacious, bootylicious butt?" Recalling their ninth grade English teacher, Ginger laughed. "How's that for alliteration? Old Mrs. Jones would be proud of me for finally understanding that." The memory of her imperious manner, coupled with gray hair, and sensible shoes made Ginger smile. "Yes, we were all terrified of her. It's a wonder we could learn anything from that, well…from that old geezer. Darn, we're as old now as she was then. Yikes. Anyway, I just had a very sobering thought."

Sandy looked long and hard at her breasts. With a gentle squeeze of her bosom, she felt a sudden appreciation of them. "We shouldn't be complaining about our breasts. At least we have them! Not all of our sisters are as fortunate."

"Well, buzz kill. You're so right. I'm sorry. We should, appreciate what we've got." Ginger embraced Sandy and kissed her on the cheek. "Thanks for reminding me of what really counts. We're alive; we're healthy; and we've still got all our body parts, even if some do jiggle like they belong on a Shar-Pei puppy."

"Right you are. We'll flaunt what we can and hide the rest." Sandy grabbed the dress that she'd selected, and put her arm through Ginger's. As they left the dressing room, Sandy said, "We're still gonna have fun. We've got a brand new appreciation of life, and nice new clothes to go along with it. A little part of me hopes that Barb Jones has gotten fat."

"Or looks much older than us," Ginger chimed in. She laughed, and hoped karma wouldn't punish them for such unkind thoughts.

* * * * *

Bubbling with enthusiasm, they left their favorite boutique. Strolling along the cobblestone street, Ginger felt young again. Obviously, Sandy did too as they giggled like two school girls. While the women window-shopped, the sun shined brightly. Only a few fluffy white 'Simpson' clouds hovered overhead.

After a few minutes, Ginger and Sandy found themselves at the entrance to Pete's Deli, one of their favorite places for lunch.

"Hey girls," Pete, the owner, called as they walked through the door. "Have a seat. I'll be right with you. You want your usual today?"

In unison, they both said, "Of course." Ginger's mouth watered while she anticipated Pete's famous pastrami on rye with his secret sauce, followed by his chocolate confection for dessert. Neither of them asked the calorie count. In less than ten minutes, Pete set their meal before them.

As she brought the first forkful to her mouth, Ginger hesitated. "Good thing we only do this about once a month, Sandy. Ahh, this is sinful, but the good kind of sin, right?" She didn't get any argument from Sandy who had already swallowed her first sinful bite.

During lunch, they continued their conversation about the reunion. Sandy held her fork in mid-air. "Do you think Sonny will come? I wonder whatever became of him with that beautiful head of hair and those movie star looks." Ginger had stopped smiling and she quickly apologized. "Oh, I'm sorry, hon. I forgot that Sonny broke your heart. That was very insensitive of me."

Ginger took a sip of her soda, and then placed the bottle on the table. She considered Sandy's question. "It's okay. I've often wondered the same thing. When he took Arleen to the prom instead of me, I wanted to die. I thought we were exclusive. Apparently, I misunderstood *his* intentions toward me."

Sandy nodded. "I think it turned out for the best. I mean, if you had continued dating him, the two of you may have gotten married. Then, you'd never have met Bill. I guess that's how we have to look at things. You think?"

"I agree. Yes, I definitely do agree. Bill was the love of my life. Although, when Sonny broke my heart, I never would have believed I could fall in love again. Sonny will always be my first love. We can never forget them, can we? Even if they break our hearts, they still occupy a special little place in our hearts."

"Yeah, like an oyster agitating a pearl." Sandy sniggered.

"You're right," Ginger cried, reaching for a napkin.

Sandy raised her bottle. "Here's to first loves and the ones who broke our hearts. May we stay forever young, and may they lose the function of certain body parts."

As Ginger sipped her drink, she burst into laughter. She covered her mouth, while tiny droplets spewed forth. "That's a hoot, girlfriend. I will most certainly drink to that." She laughed and clinked her bottle against Sandy's. A sly smile passed over her lips.

"I've always wondered if the rumors were true—that Sonny got Arleen pregnant. She was dating the other basketball star, Butch, at about the same time. Who knows? I think it's more than just rumor, though. I mean, why else would they both move right after graduation and not contact any of us again? Things were so different back then, weren't they? Today they'd just move in together, have the baby and everything would be tickety-boo."

"Ha! You're right about that. And with those movie star looks of his, I'm surprised we never saw him in any films or on TV. That was his ambition, as I recall."

Sandy lifted her sandwich to take a bite, but paused. "His cocky attitude probably kept him from getting any acting roles. He always thought he was better than everybody else just because he was so handsome. No real director would tolerate his foolishness."

"Yes." Ginger nodded. "He was cocky for sure, but he was a bit shy, too. He seemed to have two sides to him, the arrogant public persona, and the gentle, caring private boy. The person, I thought loved me."

"You give him too much credit, Ginge. He was always conceited about his flawless appearance. We can only hope he comes to the reunion, as a balding old man." Sandy giggled.

"We'll see soon enough. That is, if he even shows up. Maybe nobody could find him to tell him about the reunion or...oh, I don't even want to consider the other possibility. He may have broken my heart, but I'd still love to see him. We did have some great times before he cast me aside. But that was eons ago."

"I know, hon," Sandy patted Ginger's hand, "but I think we would've heard something if anything had happened to him. Try not to think about it. Let's pay for our food and go home. And let's hope we don't pay for it again. On our hips!" Sandy cackled.

"Not funny. My new dress won't allow even one extra inch." Using her flattened palm, Ginger pushed her plate away. "Okay, my treat today. I've got to get home. Miss Kitty gets fidgety when I'm gone too long."

Sandy smiled. "You and your cat. I don't know who dotes on whom more. Is that right, 'who dotes on whom'? Darn, where's our English teacher when I need her? Or, should I say now, when I'd actually pay attention to her? Who listens to old geezers?" The ladies snickered.

Although Sandy teased Ginger about her cat, she knew Sandy loved her as much as she did. When the waitress brought the tab, Ginger paid it. As they walked into the welcoming sunshine, they waved goodbye to Pete.

TOO YOUNG TO BE THIS OLD

CHAPTER THREE

The Reunion for the Class of 1963 finally arrived. Ginger and Sandy strolled into the beautifully decorated hotel convention room. Metallic streamers and balloons of purple and gold hung from every available surface. Ginger scanned the crowd in search of familiar faces. Sandy appeared fascinated by the way the years of extra pounds strained against the seams of the dresses worn by their former classmates, particularly the girl voted Most Popular. Ginger noticed the wrinkles that creased the cheeks of the *Prettiest Girl* in the class.

"It's a good thing they had these name badges made for everyone, or I'm sure I wouldn't know half the people here. Wait a minute. Look over there. That's Cassie Johnson, isn't it? She's really held up well. Hmmm, what a disappointment." Ginger glanced at Sandy. Amused by her findings, they both covered their sinister grins.

"I know, but we look good. Our bodies are better than hers, too." Sandy glanced around at everyone.

"Oh, Sandy," Ginger slapped Sandy's hand. "You look terrific. You always do, so stop worrying about it. By the way, I wonder where Tony is. I sure hope we didn't walk right by him. Wouldn't that be an embarrassment?"

Immediately, they headed toward the buffet table. After weeks of dieting, they looked forward to the sumptuous treats. "Boy, what little piglets we are," Sandy said, reaching for a plate. "We didn't even check our table assignment."

"Hey, Ginger!" Sandy tugged at Ginger's sleeve. "Over here. It's Tony." A loud voice boomed from the other side of the table, while Tony made his way around the end of the counter. With his right hand, he balanced his plate of food, while with his left, he reached out to Ginger. "I'd know you anywhere, Ginge." As he hugged her, he held his dish steady. "Remember, we used to always call you Ginge?"

"Some people still do, Tony." Ginger smiled, and pointed to Sandy who stood silently by. "You remember Sandy don't you? She still calls me Ginge. Apparently, she thinks we're still in high school."

Tony hugged Sandy tightly, his head almost lost in her cleavage. He scanned her from head to toe, apparently admiring her sexy dress. "You both look wonderful. You look like you're in maybe the 15th grade, no older." Tony hooted. He always chuckled at his own jokes.

"Some things never change," Ginger shook her head.

TOO YOUNG TO BE THIS OLD

Tony motioned to the table on the far left. "Come on. Let's go over to our table. I arranged for our old gang to sit together. Well, all of us who are still around, that is. Some didn't survive Vietnam, but I'm sure you already know about that. Let's have a drink and toast them while we reminisce. Gee, you girls look terrific. And I still see you as girls."

"Hey everybody, look who I found." Tony exclaimed as they approached their table. "It's Ginger and Sandy."

Tony, Ginger, and Sandy placed their plates on the beautifully decorated table. They hugged the others in the party, while exchanging hellos. After a few moments, they'd recognized everyone, except one handsome man with beautiful silver hair, pulled into a ponytail.

"You're probably wondering who this good looking man is." Tony pointed to his guest. "I'd like you to meet Ron, my partner, as in life partner." He paused, with a broad grin. "Surprised?"

Stunned, Ginger and Sandy exchanged glances. "No wonder you never asked me out, Tony," Ginger admitted. "It makes sense now."

"You were always the nicest guy in school." Sandy said. "I wish you and Ron, much happiness." Though Sandy extended her hand to Ron, he hugged her instead, pulling Ginger into the hug. "Tony has been talking about you so much, I feel like I know you. I'm very pleased to finally meet you. Tony was right. You're both beautiful."

When the band played '*In the Still of the Night*' by The Five Satins, Tony asked Ginger to dance. "Excuse me, Ron. I want to have a long-awaited dance with Ginger. It's been fifty years in the making."

As they danced, Tony explained, "I was crazy about you when we were in high school. You were like a sister to me, my best friend in fact. I wanted to tell you the truth, but back then, a guy didn't admit he was gay. I'm so glad we reconnected."

Ginger lowered her eyes bashfully. "I was always crazy about you too, Tony. I'm so glad times have changed. Now, we can all be who we are. Ron seems like a very nice man, and he's quite good looking."

"Well, he's taken." Tony laughed. "Hands off, girlfriend."

With mouth agape, Ginger felt the warmth of her cheeks. "I wouldn't dare."

When the song finished they walked back to their table. Everyone seemed to be having a wonderful time. As Tony pulled the chair from underneath the table for Ginger, Sandy asked, "What ever happened to Sonny?"

"He's probably in Europe, appearing in spaghetti westerns," someone offered.

"Or managing some third rate basketball team that nobody's ever heard of." Another voice chimed in.

Jack, a good friend from school, raised his glass to Ginger's and smiled. "He'd have one hell of a nerve if he shows his face here tonight, after ditching you for Arlene. Nobody even knew he was seeing her behind your back. That was a long time ago, though. I suppose we should just keep it in the past. Here's to you, Ginger. You made a great life for yourself with a man who deserved you. I'm just sorry he's not with us tonight."

"Thank you, Jack. You're a good friend. Excuse me. I see the dessert table, and I need a chocolate fix. Be right back." Ginger had her eye on more than the chocolates. She thought for sure she saw a man who resembled Sonny. His hair was salt and pepper, with a decidedly generous serving of salt, but it was no longer curly and full. He didn't appear quite as tall as she remembered. If this was Sonny, he'd put on several pounds—no longer the fit, trim, muscled ball player. *"Is it him, or isn't it?"*

Once Ginger made her way to the dessert table, she reached for a chocolate petit four. She summoned her courage, and elevated her eyes to the man across the table. *"Sonny,"* she thought, and smiled. Indeed, it was he. Even though he wasn't wearing a name badge, she knew it.

"Ginge? Ginger Baldwin?" Sonny's voice was mellow and smooth, just as she remembered it. That same voice had said so many tender things to her.

"I'd know you even without the name badge. It's me, Sonny." He glanced at his lapel, where his name badge should have been. "Sonny McNeill. I lost my name badge somewhere."

Ginger popped a petit four into her mouth, savoring the flavor while giving her time to think. She studied his aging but still handsome face. A swarm of butterflies fluttered in her stomach.

When Ginger finished the confection, she gave Sonny what she hoped was a friendly smile. Just friendly, nothing more. What did she say to this man who greeted her with such a platonic salutation after what they'd shared? "Hello, Sonny. You don't need the nametag for me to know who you are. And you certainly don't need to tell me your last name."

Her shoulders stiffened. "How could I forget the boy who humiliated me in front of the entire school? That's memorable. And by the way, how *is* Arleen?" Before she knew it, the words spilled forth, belying her cordiality.

Sonny dropped his jaw, along with the plate of chocolates he held. The crash brought unwanted attention to the couple. Embarrassed, Sonny averted his eyes from curious onlookers. With a wicked grin, Ginger stood quietly and glared at him.

"Well," Sonny grunted, "that's a real ice-breaker. How do I top that? Perhaps, I should build a mound of desserts, sit on them, and practice self-immolation? Would that help? Because if it would, I'd do it. Maybe you have a less painful form of penance for me?" Sonny came around the table, closing the gap between them.

"Too close for comfort," Ginger thought. It had been fifty years since she'd been that close to him. Hands shaky and knees weak, she took a deep breath. "S, sorry," Ginger stammered. "I shouldn't have blurted that out, but I've been holding it in for 50 years. Wasn't very polite of me, was it?" With furrowed brows she mused, *"Why am I apologizing to him? He's the one who needs to apologize. The concept of a funeral pyre isn't too bad either."*

Sonny moved even closer. He grasped her hand. "Ginger, there are no words to explain how awful I feel for how I treated you. All these years I've carried the guilt of what Arleen and I did. I was such a fool."

Tugging her hand from Sonny's grasp, Ginger interrupted his explanation. She held a staying hand in front of his face. "It was a long time ago, Sonny. I've had my say. Let's just let it go."

"I can't let it go, Ginge. Ginge. Your name stirs such precious memories for me. I wanted to call you so many times over the years. You don't know it, but I kept track of you."

Sonny grasped Ginger's arm, then led her to a quiet area; out of earshot of their classmates. "Let's talk over here. I have so much I need to unload. So many explanations to offer you." Ginger was speechless. "Please, sit down." He implored. "I know you don't owe me a thing..."

"You've got that right. But I'm in a generous mood tonight. I'll give you five minutes to explain why you hurt me so badly." With fire in her eyes, she added, "...not one minute more. I have an entire table of people waiting for me, and probably wondering where I am. Unlike some people, they respect my feelings."

"Oh, I suspect they watched us leave. If I know our classmates, they've scrutinized our every move." Sonny chuckled and glanced at his watch. "I'm wasting my five minutes."

Ginger shifted in her chair, anxious for an apology that was fifty years overdue. *I'll bet this is going to be a real doozy. But I have to hear it.* With a heavy sigh, she grumbled, "Go on. Time's a'wasting."

"Oh man, where do I begin? There's so much I've wanted to say to you and..."

Ginger gave him a sideways glance. "Sonny, the clock is ticking. Are you stalling? If you have something to say, please say it."

"I'm nervous, Ginge. Please cut me some slack. Okay, I'll start with the Reader's Digest version, and then I'll answer your questions with the full details. Meanwhile, I'll beg your forgiveness."

"Well, it appears you only have time for the Reader's Digest version anyway." Despite herself, she curled her lips into a smile.

"Arleen called me constantly, which stroked my ego. In short, she just threw herself at me. You know what a jerk I was in high school. I wanted it all. Believe it or not, I loved you, but..."

Ginger raised her hand, halting him. "I wouldn't *put out*, and she would. Am I right? I wasn't part of the sexual revolution. I was really innocent."

Sonny cleared his throat, and gazed at the floor. Rubbing his hands together, he continued with his explanation. "Yes, you're right. Arleen and I got together a few times. That's all it took for her to become pregnant. When I realized how much I loved you, I planned to break it off, but she told me about the baby..."

Ginger cocked her head to one side. "And you wanted to do the honorable thing, right?"

"You're wrong there. I didn't *want* to do the honorable thing; *I had to*. It's how my mother raised me. Besides, Arleen threatened to move away with the baby, and never let me see the child. She insisted I take her to the prom. What could I do? I was going to be a father, and it was such an incredible feeling. Me—a dad. My own dad died when I was just a little kid, and I didn't want my child to grow up without a father."

"Which was it?"

"Which was what?"

Ginger leaned into Sonny and placed her hand on his arm. Feeling his muscles stirred desire she hadn't felt for ten years. She inhaled deeply, and then whispered, "Which was it, a boy or a girl?"

"Oh. Well, my five minutes are already up. If you'll give me five minutes more, I'll tell you." They both snickered. How easily they laughed. "A girl. A beautiful, little girl with a button nose. You know, most people think men only want sons, but I didn't care. I really didn't. I just wanted to be a dad more than anything. I wished it could've been with you. Still, we don't always get what we want in life, do we?"

"No, but sometimes we get exactly what we deserve."

"Ouch." Sonny raised both brows pitifully.

"Why didn't you tell me? Instead, you called off our relationship with no explanation. Any reason you gave would've been better than nothing. Oh, wait. You did give me some flimsy excuse. As I recall, you said you weren't ready to be serious with *anyone*. I almost missed going to the prom, you know."

"But you did go," he pressed. "You went with Geoffrey, the English exchange student. I watched you dance with him, wishing it were me. Anyway, let me hurry this up. Arleen and I went to Maryland, married and moved in with her uncle in Baltimore. Our daughter was born there. Marielle. Marielle Marie."

"That's a beautiful name, Sonny. I'll bet she's beautiful, too."

The pride Sonny felt was evident by the enormous grin he flashed at the mention of his daughter's name. "She was a beautiful baby, and she grew into a stunning woman, both inside and out." Sonny's smile widened and his eyes brightened as he bragged about his child. "She's the shining star in my life. When Arleen left us, she's what kept me going."

Mouth agape, Ginger gasped. "What?"

"Yeah, she grew tired of being a wife and a mother. All the care of Marielle fell upon me, but I enjoyed every minute of it."

As a wistful look crossed his face, Ginger felt a resurgence of tender feelings toward him.

"For fifty years, I've held resentment toward you. I'm so sorry for your suffering."

Sonny gazed at Ginger, and smiled. "My love for my daughter far outweighs any sadness in my life. She gave me terrific twin grandsons, Michael and Matthew." He took her hand. "Enough about me. How are you doing? I told you I've kept up with you over the years. I was truly sorry to hear about Bill's passing."

Ginger frowned. "Why have you followed my life? Nobody heard from you after graduation, so how could you know what was going on with me?"

"Arleen's cousin, Caryn, stayed in touch with me through the years. She always liked me and couldn't understand how Arleen could desert her family, or her child." He shared how Caryn had called him with the latest gossip— who married whom, which couples divorced, and sadly which one of their classmates had died.

"So Caryn was your pipeline. I never would've guessed that. I haven't talked to her since graduation. The way she gossiped in high school, it's no surprise she kept up with everybody's doings."

With Ginger's hand in his, Sonny stood, gently lifting her as he did so. "You know. I would've called you, but I could never get the nerve. I wouldn't have blamed you one bit if you'd hung up on me, or worse. Then, I heard that you'd married Bill. I knew he'd be a great husband to you. Though, I must admit it broke my heart. All hope of being with you again vanished when I heard that news."

Unable to breathe, Ginger's heart fluttered as tiny drops of perspiration formed on her extremities. *"He still cares for me after all these years. If only I'd known. But what would I have done? Would I have chosen Sonny, over Bill? No, that's absurd. Sonny broke my heart. Why would I have given him a second chance?"*

Ginger flinched when Sonny uttered, "By the time I heard Bill had passed away, I was already happily remarried."

Her throat dry, Ginger stood with her hand in Sonny's. Knowing he had remarried made her heart sink. *"Why didn't he bring his wife with him to the reunion? Or, did she leave him too?"* Dreams dashed, she murmured, "I hope your second wife is much nicer to you than Arleen was. I do mean that."

"She was indeed, but she passed away last year from pneumonia. We had a good marriage, and she and Marielle got along like mother and daughter." He lifted his eyes and sighed. "I miss her."

"That's not how I envisioned her leaving him. How terribly sad. I can so relate." Ginger squeezed Sonny's hand. Her throat tight, she shed a stream of tears. "I know what it's like to

miss your mate. I'll always miss Bill. For so many years, he was such a huge part of my life. I loved him so much. So I understand how much you miss…"

"Stephanie Maxwell. Steffie. She grew up in Baltimore. We lived there until she passed away. After that, I moved back to Woodland Hills. Kept a pretty low profile. Then, I read about the reunion on Facebook, and I knew I had to come. I hoped you'd be here. Again, I didn't have the nerve to call you, but I hoped you wouldn't shun me. Mainly, I wanted to explain what happened. I'm really not an unfeeling jerk." Sonny exhaled and grinned. "Also, I thought you wouldn't beat me too badly if our meeting took place in a public setting."

"That depends on your apology, which so far, you haven't given me." Ginger narrowed her eyes suspiciously. "You've talked about it, but I still haven't received a formal, heartfelt admission of guilt. You know the get down on the floor, knife at your chest type apology. Like the dagger you stabbed through my heart. I always did have a flair for the dramatic, didn't I? So, let's dance. Isn't this one of the reasons we came to this reunion?" Ginger said with a smirk. *"I just want to feel his arms around me again, to be close to him, to feel his warmth, smell the sexy sweetness of his cologne mixed with the musky scent of his body heat."*

"No words can ever make up for what happened, Ginge. But I promise I'll do better than the knife in the chest thing." As they listened to the strains of the fifties and sixties music wafting from the ballroom, Sonny whirled Ginger around the pretend dance floor.

It had been ten years since Ginger had felt so comfortable in a man's arms. She didn't want him to let her go. Yet, a twinge of guilt threatened to overshadow her feelings of hope and anticipation. *"It's time to start living again. Time to honor my promise to Bill – that I wouldn't suspend my life because his ended. He loved me so much. How could I deny myself another chance at happiness. Time to…"*

"A penny for your thoughts." Sonny had interrupted her silent musings. "You seem miles away, or is it years away? Are you thinking about Bill? If you are, I certainly understand because Steffie still lives in my heart. She'll always live there, and Bill will always live in yours. We can't change what happened. Life is for the living. This isn't a dress rehearsal. We have to live it to the fullest."

Ginger ran her fingers through Sonny's silver hair and gazed into his deep chocolate eyes. "I don't know what lies ahead, Sonny. Or, even if I'll be sharing my life with anyone. I do know Bill would want me to move forward.

I've known it for some time, but I haven't found anyone I've wanted to take a chance with."

"That is, until tonight?" Sonny asked, with hope in his voice.

"I don't know. This is so sudden and confusing. I'd like to take a chance again. Until I saw you tonight, I didn't realize how much I've missed you."

"You know what Ginger? I've had serious doubts about the existence of heaven. But, if there isn't a heaven, how do you explain this?"

"I'd say you danced into my dream. As Bob Dylan said, '*I'll let you be in my dreams if I can be in yours.*' That's how I'd explain our meeting."

Hearing Sonny's words, Ginger felt flush. "*I'm nearly 68 years old, and he's making my cheeks blush. Can this really be happening at my age?*"

"Well then I'm so glad I did. Of all the places I could've landed, I fell smack-dab into your dream. I'd like to stay here, if you'll allow me. I've missed that beautiful smile. After all these years it still gives me goose bumps. Do you think we can take advantage of our reunion and make the most of however many years we have left? Would you like to get to know me again? Go out on a date? Stop me before I make a fool of myself. Please." He pulled her closer.

"No," Ginger gave into his touch, "don't stop. I'm enjoying it." She smiled softly. "I hope we have many years left—time to date. I'm game if you are. We'll see how things progress tonight. You must think I'm being petty and foolish. But somehow an apology, a meaningful one, would help. What's that word everyone uses today? I think it's called closure. Not sure I know exactly what that means, but I think that's the right word."

Sonny inhaled. "Yes, of course. Closure for both of us. Hold on to that thought, okay? Right now there's something more important." He wrapped both arms around her, drew her closer, and brushed his lips against hers.

With a passion Ginger hadn't felt in years, she returned his kiss. Every fiber of her being came to life. Heaven help her, she desired him as much as she had when she was an inexperienced girl. But now, she was a woman, experiencing a resurgence of passion. This time, she refused to deny herself.

They kissed for a few moments more, then caressing their bodies, they swayed to the music emanating from the ballroom. Sonny's face reddened. His desire for her was bold and apparent.

For what seemed an eternity, they danced. Conversely, it felt like mere minutes when Sonny released Ginger. He took a deep breath, then uttered, "Now let's go and face the music.

No pun intended. We should wait a few minutes though, until uh…things settle down a bit. To speed that process along, you'd better back away from me. Otherwise, we'll be here all night." He chortled.

CHAPTER FOUR

Ginger returned to the ballroom with Sonny's arm around her shoulders. Aware they were the center of attention, she felt an embarrassing warmth in her cheeks. She pointed to a large table in the center of the room. "I'm sitting at that table, with Sandy, Tony, and almost the whole gang." With the table in sight, Ginger felt her weakened knees would hardly carry her across the dance floor and to their table.

When they reached the group Sonny smiled and extended his hand to greet everyone. "I know I'm the last person you expected to see here—especially in Ginger's company. But, I hope you won't be too offended by my presence. Fifty years is a long time, and I hope our advanced years have dimmed the memories of the past." Sonny chuckled. It surprised Ginger that everyone laughed with him.

After a popular song ended, Sonny excused himself from the table. "I'll be right back. There's something I have to do."

The lyrics remained in Ginger's head, and she hummed, *"Oh my love, my darling, I've hungered for your touch a long lonely time."* She watched while Sonny talked to the bandleader. After a moment, he exchanged places with him and stood in front of the microphone.

The bandleader looked on with a broad smile while Sonny spoke into the mic. "Ladies and gentlemen of Woodland Hills High, I have a special announcement to make. You all know who I am, and you're undoubtedly surprised to see me here tonight. I know you're surprised to see me walk into the ballroom with Ginger Baldwin."

From the crowd, the room was filled with a mixture of hilarity and murmurings. People craned their necks to get a good look at Ginger.

Not knowing what to expect next, Ginger crossed her legs, and sat with her mouth agape. *"Okay, now that I'm sufficiently embarrassed, what will you say next?"*

"I'm here to make a public apology to Ginger Baldwin, for the hurt I caused her many years ago."

With tears in her eyes, Ginger gasped audibly. As she listened to Sonny's public apology, Sandy hugged her. Ginger was gratified that her best friend seemed so overjoyed for her. Happiness shared is indeed a wonderful thing.

Speaking into the mic, Sonny pointed to Ginger and continued. "I'm also here to beg your forgiveness, Ginge, and to ask for another chance. I've done a lot of growing up in fifty years. Let me prove that to you." He patted his tummy. "I've grown a bit wider too, as you can see." The crowd erupted into spontaneous laughter, and Ginger snickered along with them. "So, will you forgive me for being such a heel? Is this public admission as good as putting that knife to my chest? Because, believe me, this is one of the hardest things I've ever had to do. If you'll forgive me, I'll spend the next fifty years atoning my past indiscretions."

Again, everyone hooted, then the room was filled with applause.

Sonny wiped beneath his eye and appeared to fight back tears. "So, what do you say?" His voice cracked when he spoke. "Can you find it in your heart to accept my deepest heartfelt apology?"

Ginger got up from her seat and walked to the bandstand. One moment she smiled, then the next, she cried and extended her arms to Sonny. "Of course, I forgive you. At this time in our lives, there's no point in holding a grudge. I accept your apology. Thank you. It's way better than your putting a knife to your chest."

Cheers filled the room. Sonny held up his hand to stay the crowd, then spoke into the mic once again. Mist filled Ginger's eyes as she gazed at him. Having a mixture of awe and satisfaction, she made no effort to conceal her emotions.

"Ginger," Sonny asked, "may I have this dance?" Thumbs up, Sonny turned to the bandleader. He descended the bandstand, and took Ginger in his arms. Smiling, they glanced at their cheering classmates. Ginger loved the admiring and approving looks from their friends.

While Sonny and Ginger held each other, they looked deeply into each other's eyes She relished the second chance at love? Could it really happen?

"This song is from my heart to yours, Ginge." Sonny spoke in a low, dulcet tone. "I mean every word of it." The couple danced, as the band played an old Frank Sinatra tune. With his cheek pressed to Ginger's, Sonny sang into her ear. "…who can say what led us to this miracle we've found? There are those who'll bet love comes but once, and yet I'm oh so glad we met, the second time around…"

~The End~

I'M TOO YOUNG TO BE THIS OLD
CHAPTER ONE

*L*ate summer was Fiona's favorite part of the year. Dressed in knee length shorts, she sat on a patio recliner and watched her kittens as they romped in her prized flower garden. How youthful and carefree they appeared. She placed her soda aside, and then gazed at her aging hands. Her veins were growing larger and more apparent; new age spots made her cringe. *"Oh my. Where have the years gone?"*

Noise from the television drew her attention. Tim dearly loved his evening programs. Seemed he'd been her husband for an eternity. Had the easy chair and television taken her place in his life? *"He's always watching that screen. Never used to be that way."*

There was a time when the TV was seldom on. If it was, it served as background noise to their lovemaking. *"Those were the days,"* she thought. Their sex life had dwindled until it was virtually nonexistent. She'd lost interest in sex and everything else that once mattered to her. In truth, she'd lost interest in life.

Tim had tried to alleviate Fiona's depression — to interest her in something — anything. Yet, his efforts went unrewarded. His suggestion that she visit her doctor fell on deaf ears. She knew the problem, but admitting it meant facing her most dreaded fear — she was getting old. Age was just a number, or was it? The self-talk of her youth came back to haunt her. On her next birthday, she'd be sixty. This, she found hard to bear. Yes, age was just a number, but it was a very old number. A number she thought she'd never reach.

Judging by how quickly the years had gone by, Fiona realized she'd be seventy in no time. *"Just shoot me now,"* she screamed inwardly. *"Has my life really passed me by?"*

There were so many things she hadn't done. She'd never written the novel she told everyone she'd write by the time she was fifty. Nor, had she written the best-selling song that always danced around inside her head. Learning French had long been her goal, yet she failed mastery of that as well. Her plans to return to Dublin, Ireland, her ancestral home, fell by the wayside. Lastly, she'd never learned to tap dance. Now, the sands were falling too quickly through the hourglass for her to accomplish her aspirations.

TOO YOUNG TO BE THIS OLD

"What precisely have I done?" She'd graduated from Northwestern University with a degree in journalism, and then utilized her knowledge to gain several well-paying jobs throughout the years. It was at her alma mater where she'd met Tim, her love at first-sight romance.

When they were young, their sex life was good. Really good. Together, they raised two beautiful daughters, Molly and Annie. Both were college graduates with husbands and children of their own. Her grandchildren, Cathleen, Colleen, Ashlynne, and Liam were the lights of her life. They were the only things that brought her any joy. Now, even they couldn't bring her out of her–what was it? Was it a legitimate depression? She didn't think so. The idea of growing old bothered her. *"How many years do I have left,"* she wondered. *"Ten? Twenty? Or only a few hours? Do other women feel that way? Do they ponder such things?"* It drove her mad.

Luckily she'd brought the phone outside with her. When it rang Maria's name scrolled across the caller ID. Maria was her best friend since she and her family immigrated to the United States from Italy. The girls were ten when they met. She and Maria became fast friends, and had remained so for forty-nine years.

They made for an interesting pair. Fiona, with her auburn hair, green eyes, and light freckles, dotting her porcelain skin, had the typical rosy Irish cheeks. Maria's family hailed from Sicily, and she'd inherited her parents' olive skin, black hair, and huge brown eyes. Both girls had grown into strikingly beautiful women.

Tall and slender, Maria had carved out a successful career for herself as a print model. Fiona, short with a tiny waist, had an hourglass figure. Large breasts made her waist appear even smaller. A buxom girl, she was teased by neighborhood boys, the same lads who later pursued her.

Maria was happy and content with her life. Throughout the years she had accomplished much. On the other hand, Fiona brooded over her lack of enthusiasm about life. Unfortunately, life doesn't give a person a re-do where age is concerned. When opportunities slip away, they're gone forever.

"Fiona, before I tell you why I'm calling, please understand I won't take no for an answer. Not even a maybe. The only acceptable answer is a resounding, yes."

"No." Fiona replied, a smile tugging at her lips. "Whatever the question, the answer is, no. Put on your big girl panties and deal with it, Maria. I love you to pieces, but you know, well you know…"

"Honey, if I wore big girl panties I wouldn't still have a successful modeling career. Just listen to me. You know that song you're always talking about writing? ...the one about being too young, and old, at the same time, or something like that?"

"It's called, 'I'm Too Young to be This Old'. Well, that's what the title will be, if I ever write the lyrics. Why? What about my so-called song?"

Fiona scanned the patio and glanced back into the living room, while Tim nodded in his recliner. *"Tim doesn't look old; he's still handsome. But all he does is watch that darn television when he comes home from work. What has happened to us? Darn it. I know fifty-nine isn't considered old by other people's standards but..."*

"Fiona. Are you there? You're not listening to me. Have you zoned out on me, sweetie? I know you have, so let me say it again. And this time listen, or I'll come over there and box your ears, as you Irish people say. Or as we Italians might say, lo box le tue orecchie."

"Get on with it," Fiona teased, "but I'm going to tune you out. Don't forget, we old people don't hear very well and our minds wander. Take your best shot before I take my nap."

"I do believe you just showed a bit of humor there. That's great, because you'll need it. I just found out that the annual county Dolly

Parton look-alike contest will be held here, Hotlanta, Georgia, in six weeks. Anyone can enter — singers, songwriters. You name it."

"So? You're not suggesting that I..."

"No. No, of course not. Don't be silly."

Fiona sighed. "Well, I'm glad to hear that. You had me scared there for a minute."

"Well, don't relax, yet. I'm not suggesting, I'm telling. I've already registered us for a contest and we're going to do it. Together, we'll hammer out the songs. You'll write the lyrics, and I'll compose the music. We can do it, Fiona. It'll be a gas, a real hoot. Even if we don't win, we'll have fun. That's something you've been sorely lacking for quite a while. I just know the song will lift your spirits."

Fiona shook her head. "I'm not making any promises, but come over tomorrow morning about nine, and we'll discuss it. That's all I'm open to right now."

"Ciao," Maria said, hanging up the phone.

"Ciao," Fiona repeated to herself. She hung up the phone and walked into the living room. Eventually, Tim would go upstairs without even saying good night. *"What have I done to him? He deserves so much more than I've given him. Perhaps, I should put some words to paper, anything to get Maria off my back."*

CHAPTER TWO

That evening, Fiona walked into her home office and sat at her desk. She turned on her computer, read some emails, and then forced herself to type. Even if the words were nonsense, she'd at least try. Maria and Tim would have to give her credit for the attempt.

"Fiona? Fee?"

Hearing her name being called, Fiona opened her eyes. She raised her head as it rested upon her arms.

"What's going on?" Tim demanded, leaning against the doorframe. "You haven't been to bed all night, have you?" He marched into her office, where she sat hunched over her desk.

"Oh, Tim," Fiona wiped her bleary eyes. "I'm sorry. I didn't mean to worry you. You see, Maria entered us in the Dolly Parton look-alike contest. I've been up all night writing the words to a song. Fiona knew her confession would surprise Tim. She felt upbeat and confident, certain he'd notice her new attitude. It had been too long since she'd felt enthusiastic about anything.

Tim folded his arms. "When do I get to hear this song?" His eyes were aglow as he made his next statement. "I don't want to push you, or make you nervous. Truthfully, it's like I'm seeing a new Fee."

The wall clock drew Fiona's attention and she gasped. "Maria will be here in... Good grief it's 8:45. She'll be here in about fifteen minutes. I've gotta brush my teeth and make some coffee."

"You brush your teeth, and I'll put the coffee on. Would a good morning kiss be too much to ask for?"

Fiona stood, hugged her husband, and gave him a feathery kiss before she rushed upstairs to the bathroom. Old feelings stirred inside her. *"Baby steps, Fiona,"* she told herself. Other than that wee kiss, there wasn't time for anything else with Tim. The drill sergeant was on her way.

* * * * *

Clean and dressed for the day, Fiona descended the stairs, just as Tim opened the front door for her friend. *"Glad I stayed focused on getting dressed."*

"Hey, Maria. Come on in," Tim greeted cordiality. Whispering to Maria, he said, "I think she'll be cooperative. Don't ask. You'll see."

"Hey, I heard that." Reaching the last step, Fiona folded her arms. "You two should work on your stage whisper. Maria, come into my office. Have I got something to show you. Get your piano fingers warmed up, girl. I think we have a hit in the making. I know you can't tell by how gorgeous I look; so refreshed and all."

TOO YOUNG TO BE THIS OLD

"Yeah, I can tell." Maria ran her gaze along Fiona's freshly shampooed hair. "Just look at those bags under your eyes. You're a real knockout. 'Sei un vero knockout', as we'd say in Italian. What'd you do? Stay up drinking last night?"

"Spoken like a true friend," Fiona placed her hand on Maria's shoulder, "my fine Italian meatball. No, I spent the night writing the song. I'll recite the lyrics, but the music is your department."

"Let's hear it. The melody will depend on the words."

Fiona printed two copies of her song, and they discussed the emotions she wanted to convey. Maria would take care of the tune on her piano when she got home.

Maria gave Fiona a big hug. "I can't wait to see you in your Dolly wig and makeup. You're going to look fabulous. Even if we don't win, we'll still have fun, won't we? It's so nice to see you upbeat again."

Fiona smiled warmly, and kissed Maria's cheek. "Writing that song last night made me realize what an idiot I've been. I'm not old. I have plenty of living to do. Tim even kissed me this morning. It made me yearn for the old Fiona. It was like a light bulb going off over my head. I want me back."

CHAPTER THREE

The night of the contest arrived. Tim was already dressed and waiting for Fiona downstairs. As she walked into the room, he gasped, "Oh my! You take my breath away, Fee. If I didn't know better, I'd swear I'm looking at the real thing. With that blonde wig and those luscious red lips, you look more like Dolly Parton, than Dolly Parton. He scanned her from head to toe. "Your outfit couldn't be made of more than one yard of material. I must say, it fits your curves in all the right places. I'd better hold you tight, so you don't fall off those sky-high heels. You're dazzling." He softened his voice. "And you're mine."

When Fiona and Tim arrived at the venue, Maria was already waiting. Bubbling with excitement, she uttered, "You're positively gorgeous. You *are* Dolly. Guess what? We're the last act. Can you believe that? We'll be the last thing on the judges' minds."

Two hours later, the emcee announced the last act of the evening. "Ladies and gentlemen, our last Dolly contender is Fiona Smith, singing an original composition, written especially for this contest. Accompanying Dolly on the piano is Maria Martino. Here they are, singing, 'I'm Too Young to be This Old.'

As Fiona took the stage, the crowd applauded. She definitely resembled Dolly more than any of the others. While Maria played, *I'm Too Young To Be This Old*, Fiona sang and danced; imitating Dolly perfectly.

♪ "Skinny jeans and belly shirts, they tell me I shouldn't wear

'Cause once you pass a certain age, some parts you shouldn't bare

But I look good for my age, so I'm often told

So why do I feel this rage? Because I'm too young, to be this old.

Too young to be this old, too old to feel this young.

And if the truth be told I'm still havin' lots of fun

'Cause women of a certain age have many talents untold

So come on sisters sing with me, we're too young to be this old

Too young to buy new shoes for fit, instead of for the style

♪Too young to sit at home, instead of goin' out and goin' wild

Too young to be ignored, and put into a mold

Too young to be cast aside, I'm too young to be this old

I wanna wear my clothes too tight, and skirts slit up to there

Just like I did years ago, and nobody seemed to care

But now you look at me like silver, instead of gold

Where oh where did my life go? I'm too young to be this old

Too young to be this old, too old to feel this young

And if the truth be told, I'm still havin' lots of fun

'Cause women of a certain age have many talents untold

So come on sisters sing with me, we're too young to be this old

I still think and feel the same, my desires have not gone cold

Good lookin' men still turn my head, 'cause I'm too young to be this old

Too young to be this old, too old to feel this young

I need more time to live my life, my song has not been sung

So come on sisters sing with me, let's rise up and be bold

We're valuable and beautiful, and we're too young to be this old

Too young to be this old, too young to be this old." ♫

By the time Fiona finished her song, the audience gave her a standing ovation, in a clapping frenzy. The crowd begged for an encore, which the emcee allowed.

Amid thunderous applause, the judges declared Fiona the winner. She thanked everyone, including her partner, Maria Martino—her loving husband Tim, and especially Dolly. Overcome with emotion, this was the most satisfying moment of her life. As a deep love for her husband washed over her, she regretted the distance she had allowed to form between them.

During the drive home, Fiona cuddled against Tim's large frame. While they listened to their favorite radio station, she rested her head on his shoulder. With her right hand, she caressed his thigh. She loved the familiarity of her actions; the warmth she felt while watching Tim's reaction. It had been a great night, and the evening would only get better.

Tim placed his hand on Fiona's cheek. "I've missed your touch more than you know, Fiona. When we get home, we'll make up for lost time. But it's not going to happen if you cause me to have an accident."

"Okay, I'll be good," she flirted, "but it's going to be hard." Happy to be close to her husband again, Fiona snuggled against Tim.

"You know, Fee, your song could be on the radio one day. Who knows where this win tonight might lead? I don't know if I can come up with enough adjectives to describe your performance tonight. I'm so proud of you. I love you very much. I've missed you."

Fiona kissed Tim's neck. "I don't know what got into me. Maybe, I read too many magazine articles about preserving your youth—how to look young, stay young, and reverse the signs of aging. I should have read books on how to grow old gracefully, accept who I am, and be happy with myself. I bought into the whole youth concept. I'm so sorry and I'm so glad you didn't leave me. I was…"

Pulling the car into the driveway, Tim shushed her. "I'll admit I didn't know what to do—how to handle the situation. I crawled into my own little shell, because you were no longer there. But you're back. We both are. I think it's time we got on the bicycle again, don't you?" Tim leaned over, gathered her in his arms, and kissed her. He murmured, "Let's go in the house. Some fine champagne and a big comfortable bed await us. You're not old my beautiful Fiona. You're vital and alive. Who knows what you'll accomplish next? Let's live for now. You're just a kid of fifty-nine, and you're too young to even think about being old. Hey! That sounds similar to a great song I heard tonight."

Tim smiled, and Fiona's spirits soared. She was definitely back.

~The End~

A TORCH FOR DANIEL
CHAPTER ONE

$\mathcal{M}$onica read the words with a curious mixture of empathy and anticipation. The last name, Donohue, pricked the hairs on the back of her neck. After twenty years apart from Daniel Tanner, she was under no obligation to attend his brother-in-law's funeral. However, she knew she'd never forgive herself if she didn't attend the services for Ray.

Would her flames for Daniel ignite once again? She didn't want to spend another minute thinking about it. All those years, she'd lived with glowing embers of their ill-fated relationship. Unrelentingly, they'd smoldered within her heart. Had it been the same for Daniel, or were there others after she left the picture?

Years with Daniel had ruined her life. She tried to move forward, dating a few men here and there. Sure, she got married, but divorced was unavoidable. Her heart always belonged to Daniel Tanner. Memories of their love had kept her going through rough times.

Throughout the last twenty years, Monica's daydreams had been consumed with memories of their lovemaking. She couldn't ponder those times without the word torrid popping up. Theirs was indeed a hot romance.

Monica missed awakening to her very own special alarm clock, Daniel. Still naked from a night of passion, Daniel would shake her gently, and then urge her to get ready for work.

Depending on her mood, that alarm clock had one big drawback, or advantage. It had awakened her half an hour too early each day. Most of the time, her mood had matched Daniel's. They'd make love so long she'd almost be late for work.

"Those were the days." She sighed. *"I miss Daniel so much. His lips, his hands, his strong arms, his...well...I miss every wonderful part of him."*

The familiar ring of her cell phone interrupted Monica's thoughts. She folded the paper, placed it on the kitchen counter, and then picked up the phone. "Hi, Sis. I know why you're calling."

Mandy's voice was solemn. "So, you saw it too, huh? I just read the notice in the paper. I know you'll want to go. Want me to go with you? I don't want you to go alone."

Monica placed her coffee mug in the microwave, then sat at the kitchen table to wait. "You're right. I'm going, but I'm going alone. Thanks for offering, though. I'll be fine. At least, I hope so. Reading the obits got me thinking about a lot of things. You know, Mandy, I never really got to know Daniel's brother-in-law. The few times we spoke, I found him warm and kind. Had Daniel and I stayed together, I'm sure Ray and I would have become good friends. It's sad we didn't get the chance. Daniel would have liked that. It's too late now, though."

"We can't live in the past. For our sanity, we have to move on and forget regrets. Daniel was responsible for your breakup. Then again, perhaps we can't blame him completely. The alcohol fueled his behavior. Look at the great job he had, the best radio personality in all of Seattle. What a shame."

A wistful smile passed over Monica's face as she recalled the first time she'd heard the dulcet tones of his voice on WSAT. "He had it all, Mandy. I don't think there was a woman in Seattle who didn't want him. He might have been on radio, but that impish smile was plastered all over Seattle; from billboards to TV ads."

"Not to mention all the TV fundraisers he did for the children's home, and our humane society. He had the most recognizable face in Seattle."

"Let's not forget his participation in the annual bachelor charity event. If you recall, he was the most sought after bachelor every year. All those lucky ladies bid tons of money for him, but that was before we met. Daniel assured me later they got only what they paid for. One date. He's a sexual animal, so I had my doubts about that one date thing. That was in the past, and it was better left there. The maxim of a leopard not changing his spots could apply to Daniel as well. His past will always be in the back of my mind."

Mandy's voice livened. "I heard rumors, too, but that's what they were—rumors. I never heard anything concrete about those dates. Like you said, it's all in the past. We should leave it there."

The microwave beeped, and Monica withdrew her coffee. She grabbed a granola bar from her pantry, unwrapped it, and took a bite. Crunching on the treat, she took a sip of her coffee. "I think I always knew his jet-set lifestyle would backfire on him, sis. Remember how he loved to show off his status by tooling around town in one of his expensive cars? That high-speed car crash didn't deter his wild ways. It was a stroke of luck that he hadn't been drinking when the accident happened.

Had the incident occurred after he'd left the bar, it would have been a different ballgame."

CHAPTER TWO

Under a drizzly Seattle sky, Monica drove to the funeral home. January raindrops skittered across the windshield, increasing as she drove. Luck was with her. As she approached the funeral chapel, she found an empty parking space. With an anxious heart, she told herself. "Okay, I can do this. Take deep breaths and relax."

Monica didn't know why she held such high hopes. She turned the rear view mirror to check her make-up, and then tossed her blonde mane across her shoulders.

She'd stuffed her feelings deep inside the basement of her heart, or so she thought. That night, emotions left the basement and ascended to the top floor. With each breath, they rose rapidly to the penthouse.

Mourners hurried into the building, dodging puddles that had accumulated on the sidewalk. As Monica watched the passersbys, she knew it was now or never. It was time to join the crowd and pay her respects. She'd see if there was still a spark left for him. Could such a spark reignite a dormant fire?

Dozens of thoughts swept through her mind. How could two people have such an out-of-this-stratosphere love life, and yet, give it away? They were so young when they were together. All that mattered was sex.

Apparently, that was the only foundation they'd had, but what a basis. Monica smiled at the memories and yearned for a repeat performance. Though years had passed, Daniel still had a stranglehold on her.

Monica had been helping with the *Paws and People* adoption booth in the convention center the day she met Daniel. She seemed to be the only female in town who wasn't impressed by his possessions and celebrity status. He pursued her for weeks after their initial meeting. Finally, he convinced her to give him a chance. Daniel's reputation had made her wary. There was no way she wanted to be another notch on his belt.

Rushing back from her daydream, Monica checked the time on the amethyst and diamond-encrusted watch Daniel had given her. His words still echoed in her heart. "Every second that ticks away, represents how often I think of you."

As she sat in the car, she summoned her courage to face the love of her life. *"I'll bet he won't even notice that I still wear it. Will he even remember giving it to me?"*

There was still time to join the other mourners in the funeral parlor. A small group of people stood outside the building. Monica shook her head as she observed the so-called lamenters. Some laughed; others enjoyed a last minute smoke.

Monica took a deep breath. Once again, she checked her hair and makeup in the visor mirror. *"This rain is going to ruin my hair. By the time I get inside, I'll look like a hag. Darn. Sometimes I hate Seattle."*

She picked up her umbrella from the passenger side floor. As she opened the car door, she poked the umbrella outside, clicked it open, and slid off the seat. Holding the parasol over her head, she closed and locked the door. Much to her displeasure, the rain fell in steady streams.

"Of course, it couldn't wait until I get inside the building, could it? Murphy's Law! Then again, I shouldn't have sat in the car as long as I did. Serves me right."

Monica braced herself, ran across the street, and entered the foyer of the funeral home. Umbrellas were bunched together in a large Victorian stand. Her hands trembled as she added her own wet parasol to the others. Waiting in line behind the other people, Monica listened to the funeral dirge.

"Mental note: There will be no doleful music at my funeral. In fact, there will be no funeral at all. Cremation is best for me. I want my life celebrated. Dance on my favorite beach, or park. Friends can scatter my ashes to the wind, or disperse them into the sea. It doesn't matter."

She looked at the quiet group around her, then wondered if they shared her ideas as well. *"Probably not. They look like a sensible bunch."*

Unable to control her hands, Monica signed the guest book with a shaky scrawl. After giving the pen to the gentleman behind her, she gave a sigh of relief. *"At least one part of the ordeal is finished."* Unsteady with emotions, she turned and walked inside the chapel.

Scanning the mourners' faces, Monica caught her breath. Her throat constricted so tightly she feared she'd choke. *"How would they handle another corpse in the room?"* Despite the dread in her heart, she chuckled. *"Wipe the smile off your face, Monica."*

Monica elevated her eyes toward the front of the sanctuary. As expected, Daniel was there. He wasn't only there, he was there with *her* — his ex-wife, his *first* ex-wife, to be precise. Two others had come after wife number one, and in rapid succession. None of the three had lasted more than two years. At least, she had lasted five years.

His beautiful silver hair was much shorter than she remembered. Wearing an expensive suit, crisp white shirt and a black silk tie, he was the picture of elegance. His six-foot frame carried an additional fifteen to twenty pounds. At five-nine, Monica was a good physical match for him.

"Why is his first ex here? Why not the others? That's funny. I never considered that any of them might be here tonight. Wow. I was so caught up in my own drama, I didn't think of anyone else — too concerned with what Daniel would think of me."

She moaned. *"No. I was too busy wondering how he'd react when he saw me. How would he treat me? Am I so shallow, that everything revolves around me? I feel like scum. Really. I do feel sympathy for Laura. Ray's gone and she'll be all alone. Daniel said they married fresh out of high school. Poor thing. I can't imagine what she must be feeling."*

There were more immediate concerns, however. What should she do? If she attempted to sneak out, would he see her? Monica's heart fluttered, and her ears rang. Her legs wouldn't hold her much longer; she needed to find a wall for support. Though Monica's eyes were drawn to Daniel, she had to escape. Like driving by a traffic accident, she didn't want to look, but some unfathomable emotion compelled her to do so.

Monica didn't think Daniel had seen her. For that, she was grateful. As long as Daniel didn't look in her direction, she could admire his handsome features and fantasize about their time together. In an instant, his next actions broke her spell. He slipped his arm around his ex's waist, and broke her heart yet again. *"Her fat waist,"* she noted. Monica reprimanded herself for being so petty and mean-spirited. To assuage her conscience, she reasoned she was acting out of envy. Because she possessed a rather thin frame, Monica never judged people by appearances.

"Why is he embracing her, though? Are they a couple again? What does she have that I don't?"

As Monica leaned against the wall in a far corner, she saw Daniel's ex-wife kiss him. It was a brief kiss, *but still*. It was a kiss and he didn't appear to resist.

An older woman, who was standing beside Monica, reached inside her purse. After a few moments, she withdrew a tissue and offered it to Monica. "Yes," she said, with a sniffle. "It's so sad, isn't?" Obviously, she had noticed the tears that trickled down Monica's face.

The kind stranger had no idea how truly sad it was. "Yes, it is sad. So very, very sad. Thank you." Monica blotted her tears. Before the stranger could engage in further conversation, she excused herself, and headed for the door.

Her heels clicked noisily against the tiled floor. It was imperative to make her escape without incident. "Oh, my God, I signed the guest book." Monica didn't realize she'd uttered the words aloud.

The man in front of her turned around. "Excuse me?"

With an apologetic smile, Monica looked away. The gentleman resumed his exit. Extricating herself from that mess would be tricky. Tomorrow. She'd worry about it tomorrow. Because she didn't lie well, Monica would have to give the situation a great deal of thought.

"Surely, I can devise some plausible explanation for not staying – a migraine, an urgent phone call, anything." How could she admit the green-eyed monster had reared its ugly head?

Deep in thought, Monica walked into the foyer. Trying not to make eye contact with anyone, she retrieved her umbrella from among many. To her relief, she reached the door and made an exit without incident. Though the rain came down in buckets, she decided she'd rather be soaked than humiliated.

Monica walked through the puddles with a quick stride. The rain fell in sheets, and strong winds made the umbrella useless. A sidestep would have spared her new, expensive shoes. At that moment, her shoes were the least of her worries. She couldn't believe she'd just thought that. At any other time, those words would have never entered her thoughts.

Reaching the car, Monica retrieved her keys and unlocked the door. She closed her umbrella, tossed it into the back seat, and threw herself into the car.

"Whew! I made it." She was wringing wet, but that beat an encounter with Daniel and, what's-her-name. The first Mrs. Ex.

Wet, and angered by the moment, Monica spent a few moments, drying herself. Rain dripped from her hair. A quick survey of her face in the visor mirror, revealed what she'd suspected — raccoon eyes.

"So much for expensive water-proof mascara."

CHAPTER THREE

Monica put the key into the ignition and started the car. She looked over her left shoulder to check for traffic. As she turned her head, a thumping on the passenger window unnerved her, and she gasped.

Outside her window, Daniel stood in the rain, holding an umbrella. She couldn't believe her eyes. "Monica," he yelled, above the crashing rain. "I thought that was you. Please, unlock the door. I'd like to come inside."

Well, there was no escaping it. She wouldn't need to conjure flimsy excuses. Her mother's words leapt into her mind. *"Always tell the truth, Monica Anne. Lies will give you ulcers."* Monica narrowed her eyes. *"Yeah, Mom, that and the Helicobacter pylori bacterium. Let's not forget that."*

With a click, Monica unlocked the passenger door. Daniel opened it, threw his umbrella in the back seat, and hopped inside.

Wonderment played across his familiar face. A small grin sat beneath his widened eyes. Was he unsure of his next words? "Monica, I...I'm shocked. Really, I shouldn't be. I knew you'd come. Somehow, I just knew you'd be here for me. Do you know how much your thoughtfulness means to me?"

Her mouth became dry; her stomach felt as if it were in her throat. She swallowed. "I had to come, Daniel. I knew you'd expect me. Yes, I wanted to be here for you."

"Why didn't you stay? Did you even look for me?" Daniel shifted in his seat, and then leaned closer to her.

Monica moistened her parched lips. "My first instinct is to lie, but the truth is, I saw you with your ex-wife and…"

"You saw her kiss me. Am I right?"

Monica lowered her head. "Yes."

"It was just a friendly kiss, nothing more. If you had stayed, I would have acquainted you with Rachel's husband, Craig. I introduced them. They're very happy, and I'm happy for them."

Elated, Monica sat up straight. She gave him a look that indicated she didn't believe him. "Why did you put your arm around her waist? That was an affectionate move."

Continuing to gaze into Monica's eyes, Daniel chuckled. "Yes. There was affection in that hug. We're still friends. You don't miss much, do you? You never did. Long ago, Rachel and I discovered that we make better friends than spouses, so we've remained friends. That's all there is to it. End of story."

Relieved, Monica relaxed and gazed at Daniel. "I believe you. You've never lied to me. Of course, a lot of things can happen in twenty years. Maybe you've changed." She didn't bother to mention her thoughts about the dreaded leopard and his spots.

"Yes. I have changed. I'd like to think I've changed for the better." Daniel's hazel eyes rested on Monica. "Would you get upset if I hugged you?"

Monica didn't know why, but she moved from his grasp. Was she afraid of getting hurt again? "Daniel." Monica hesitated. "Since when did you start asking *me* for what I want?"

He sighed, and leaned closer. Placing his left hand on her shoulder, he squeezed lightly. "You still haven't answered me, Monica."

"Do I have to? I think you know the answer."

Daniel pulled her closer, kissed her, and then whispered in her ear. "I've missed you so much." He held her for what seemed an eternity.

With equal enthusiasm, Monica returned his embrace. For far too long, her arms had been empty. It felt so right. She sighed. "Seems like forever."

"Too long," Daniel murmured, as he stared into her eyes. Apparently, drinking in her presence, Daniel seem to admire her; savoring every drop.

"Do I pass your inspection? I'm twenty years older now." While Monica fidgeted, she pulled stray hairs off her cheek, and then ran her fingers through her damp hair.

"And you're every bit as beautiful as you were back then. There're a few wisps of gray in your beautiful honey-blonde hair; that's all. I'm glad you didn't dye it. It looks good with your gorgeous green eyes. If anything, you're even more beautiful now."

Monica laced her fingers through her hair, separating the strands. "Thank you. I see that over the years you've learned how to pay compliments. I'm not sure mentioning my gray hair is such a flattering remark. But, I'll ignore that statement, and concentrate on the *beautiful* part."

Daniel stroked her arm. "I'm sorry. That wasn't very gallant of me. I was struck by how gorgeous you are. Gray hair notwithstanding. Even if you were bald, you'd still be the most desirable woman I've ever known."

"Compliment accepted." Monica kissed him tenderly on the cheek. "I'm so sorry about Ray. I know how much you'll miss him."

A forlorn expression crossed Daniel's face, and sympathy welled inside Monica.

"Thanks, Monica. As you know, Ray and I were close. He was more like a brother to me than an in-law. Would you mind if we went back inside for a few minutes? My sisters are probably wondering where I am. It'll only take a couple of minutes. I know we look like we just went swimming, but..."

"Let's do it," Monica replied. "I'll feel better if I can pay my respects to your sisters, especially Ray's wife. I know how difficult this must be for her." She paused. "And Daniel... Never mind, we'll talk later, okay?"

Funerals were so difficult for Monica. She hated them and vowed she'd never subject her family and friends to one. To anyone who would listen, she declared she wanted her life celebrated with a band playing, people dancing, and storytelling—good, bad, or funny. There should be no doom or gloom.

The couple grabbed their umbrellas, and exited the car. They sprinted back to the funeral chapel. After leaving their parasols in the foyer, they walked into the main viewing room. Daniel grabbed Monica's hand as if she were his lifeline. He navigated through the crowd. His brother-in-law was also in the media and almost as popular as Daniel. It seemed that half of Seattle turned out for his funeral, and most of the people remained inside.

They found Daniel's sisters and spoke with them. Monica didn't know them well, but they seemed pleased to see her. Plus, they were gracious enough not to comment on their bedraggled state. During the entire exchange, Daniel never released Monica's hand. As the minutes ticked by, she grew more anxious. She needed to escape the oppression of the dismal atmosphere. Strengthened, she resolved she would not exit life in the same depressing fashion. *"Bring on the music, please! Tell a joke. Please say something funny about Ray. Let's lift up our hearts and make a joyful noise. Where's the Dixieland music? Ray would probably love that."*

As Monica gazed at Daniel, she felt as if time stood still. The preceding twenty years were more like a blip on the radar screen. Her happiness for their reunion was marred only by the circumstances.

For more than fifteen minutes, Daniel and Monica consoled Laura, his sister-in-law. He shook hands with mourners, and accepted their sincere condolences. Finally, the time came to exchange the heavy atmosphere for the lighter feel of the coffee house across the street. They excused themselves, and Daniel promised his sisters he'd see them later. Monica didn't see the first Mrs. Ex anywhere. Of course, she wasn't looking very hard.

CHAPTER FOUR

Outside, Monica and Daniel continued their conversation with ease. They both stepped into the drizzling rain. Monica, with a light heart and high hopes, wondered if Daniel felt the same. Why bother to open the umbrellas? They were both soaked. Daniel placed his arm around Monica's waist while guiding her across the street. Under the cover of the coffee shop's awning, he kissed her ever so gently. Slowly, Daniel withdrew his lips from hers, and gazed into her eyes. It was a look she remembered well, pure animal lust. How she'd missed the rawness of his desire.

A couple exiting the shop opened the door, and the aroma of coffee wafted outside. Daniel inhaled. "I've missed kissing you. I've missed everything about you, and our life together. I can't believe I'm actually standing here with you."

Steering Monica out of the way of passing patrons, Daniel pulled her closer. He enveloped her in his strong arms, and smothered her lips, kissing her urgently. Pent up passions were released in an explosion of bliss. It felt so natural, yet, so oddly unnatural. All she knew was that her emotions felt right.

How Monica hoped he'd changed his domineering ways in the intervening years. She knew he never meant to control her. He only needed to assert himself in what he considered a traditional man/woman relationship. The consumption of alcohol intensified his arrogance. She believed in equality and would not accept drunkenness as an excuse for egotistical behavior.

As if it had happened yesterday, Monica found herself remembering one of their last conversations. "Daniel," she'd said. "Sometimes the man takes control, and sometimes it's the woman."

"There can be only one captain of a ship, Monica," he'd said.

"Good point, but you've never accepted that sometimes the captain can be a woman." Because of her submissive behavior, Monica realized she shared the blame for allowing him to control the rudder, but that was then.

Reluctantly, they released each other, and entered the coffee house. A server ushered them to a small table in the back of the room. Happy voices of exuberant patrons competed with the lone melody of a strumming guitarist. Daniel placed their wet umbrellas on an empty chair at their table.

Before Monica had a chance to sit, Daniel pulled her chair out, waited for her to get comfortable, and then eased into the chair opposite hers.

A bouncy young waitress, who appeared to be college age, hustled over to their table. In her arms, she carried two kitsch coffee cup-shaped menus. However, that didn't matter to Monica. For all she cared, the menu could have been printed on paper towels. The attractive server placed the menus on the table, and smiled. "Hi, there. I'm Kariann. Would you like a few minutes to look at the menu?"

Daniel spoke up, which was no surprise. "Well, hi there, Kariann. I'm Daniel," and pointing to Monica he added, "and this beautiful lady is Monica."

The attendant giggled. In a saucy manner, she placed one hand on her hip. "You're the man in the TV commercials, right? Daniel Tanner. Your face is stuck on every billboard in Seattle. I think this is the first time you've visited our shop. Sorry for being so chatty. Anyway, it's nice to meet you, Daniel, and you too, Monica."

Monica shook her head at Daniel, and flashed an apologetic smile at the server. In twenty years, he hadn't lost his playful nature. "Don't pay any attention to him, Kariann. He's always had a weird sense of humor."

"And she's missed it," Daniel said, giving Monica a sly look. He shifted his attention back to the server. "I think we'll have coffee for now. A nice strong coffee will do me just fine. None of those girly dessert coffees for me. How about you, Monica? You still like those girly drinks?" Grinning, he gave Monica what she perceived to be a look of pleasant recollection.

Monica shrugged. "I suppose some things never change." She smiled sweetly. Daniel's grin grew broader, seemingly he was satisfied that he still knew her likes and dislikes. "Tonight, I think I'll join you in a regular coffee." Her smile grew wider. *"This is the new and improved Monica. Not the old pushover who wouldn't stand up, or fight for herself."*

Monica turned to face Kariann. "Don't make mine too strong, please." She crossed her arms and leaned forward to place them on the table, and then she looked directly into Daniel's eyes. *"I wonder what he thinks of the new Monica."*

Kariann wrote their orders on a pad and said, "Very good. A wise choice not to have fancy coffees. Tonight we have fresh Mississippi Chocolate Mud Pie on the menu. It's worth every sinful calorie. May I bring you some?"

Before Monica could decline the decadent treat, Daniel answered again. "Yes. We'll both have a slice." He raised both brows in question. "If that's okay with you?"

"If that's okay with me? Did he just say what I thought he said? Has he mellowed?" Monica sat back in the chair, and crossed her legs. "Why not? We could both use some extra serotonin and dopamine tonight. What better way to

deliver that than in a delicious chocolate dessert?"

Kariann reached for the menus and bubbled. "You won't be sorry, Monica. Trust me. I'll be right back with your coffee and pie. I'm sure you'll enjoy both, especially the pie." She turned quickly and headed toward the kitchen.

After Kariann left their table, Daniel took Monica's hands in his. He caressed them, and then kissed her palms. How she'd missed those kisses. No one could kiss like Daniel. No one else thrilled her like he did, yet no one had ever hurt her so badly.

"Monica," Daniel murmured, his eyes misting. He shifted in his seat and hung his head before he continued. "You have no idea how much it means that you came here tonight. I treated you terribly. For that, I'm sorry. I don't know if I can explain my actions. How can I make you understand the way I felt, or why I cheated?" He shrugged. "Why I ended our affair. You were the love of my life." His voice softened. "You still are."

Daniel gazed into her eyes before continuing. "I was too young for a serious relationship. Commitment and responsibility were foreign concepts to me. At the time, I was scared, but I couldn't admit that to you," he muttered, "or myself. All I cared about was sex, and lots of it. I had no idea what a real relationship should be. I hate to admit it, but attention from women fed my ego. Women were falling at my feet, praising my every move. My life wasn't as easy as it seemed. It took me a long time to grow up."

Monica looked wistfully at Daniel. "Me too, I suppose. It took a long time to learn how to be strong."

"Throughout the years, you'll never know how many times I picked up the phone to call you. For fear of rejection, I'd lose my resolve."

A familiar melody drew Monica's attention. The guitarist slowed the tempo with some old Eric Clapton tunes. Clapton was Daniel's favorite artist and hers as well. When the musician strummed *Wonderful Tonight*, Daniel sang along softly. As he stared at Monica, tears filled his eyes. Other patrons were singing and swaying in time to the music.

The melody enraptured Monica. It had been their song. Never had it sounded as sweet as it did that night. She waited until Daniel finished his serenade before she said, "Daniel, I understand. I really do. We were young, immature and randy." Embarrassed, she felt her cheeks redden. Memories of their enthusiastic sex life flashed before her eyes, particularly Daniel's touch and romantic nature.

"I'm happy you still remember our song. You do look wonderful tonight. Thank you for not laughing at my sentimentality."

Monica choked up as she responded, "How could I laugh at you? I love your sentimentality. Real men aren't ashamed to be sentimental, nor do they fear expressing genuine emotion. I've always admired that about you, that, and your kindness."

Kariann arrived with their coffees. After placing the cups on the table, she went to the kitchen for the pie. When she returned, she placed the pie on the table, reached inside her apron pocket, and then pulled out two napkins. Each contained a knife and fork. "Enjoy. Let me know if you need anything else, or when you want your check." Before moving to the next table, she smiled.

If the pie tasted as good as it looked, Monica knew she'd experience chocolate heaven. She didn't know about Daniel, but her stomach was churning. Hopefully, she could eat her pie, and keep it down. They each took a sip of coffee.

"Monica." Daniel cleared his throat. "When I heard you'd married Darren," he hesitated, "I spiraled into some sort of depression. I found refuge in Jack Daniels and Johnny Walker, again. They were my only companions for years. That is, until I discovered Xanax. Then, I had more friends to help me get through the nights. Truthfully, I don't understand why I'm not dead. It wasn't for lack of trying." Daniel averted his eyes from Monica for a few moments. "Sometimes, I'd drive by your office at quitting time, hoping to catch a glimpse of you. Other times, I'd sit in the parking lot and wait. I know. I was pathetic. That's what booze and drugs will do to you. They take over your mind and body. They're in complete control."

Monica ran her hand down his arm, and then held both his hands. "Daniel. You stubborn cuss. I'm so sorry. I had no idea you were fighting such an addiction. I didn't know you cared that much. There was no way I could know. When you decided you weren't interested in our relationship, we parted. You never contacted me. I picked up the pieces of my life, and tried to put them back together. It wasn't easy."

Daniel poked the pie with the side of his fork. He cut off a healthy chunk, and lifted it to his mouth. Then, without taking a bite, he put his fork down. "I really made a mess of it, didn't I? When I heard you and Darren had divorced, I decided to straighten up and fly right. You didn't know I kept such close tabs on you, did you?" I realized there was no way I'd ever have a chance with you again, if I was drinking. Adding pills to the mix was toxic. Before I faced you, I knew I had to be sober.

Monica widened her eyes in disbelief. "You actually stalked me at the medical clinic? I had no idea. That's kind of scary. I'll have to be more aware of my surroundings from now on." Her nervous laugh covered a deeper thought.

"You might not know it, but you almost scared me straight. Once, I waited for you in the parking lot. You didn't show up. I thought you'd taken the day off. The next day, you weren't there either. I hoped you had taken some vacation days. When another week passed without my seeing you, I went into a full-blown panic. I thought perhaps you'd moved away. My alcohol consumption clouded my memory of those days. Finally, I swallowed my pride and called my friend, Rose. She told me you were still in town, but working from home. You have no idea how happy I was to hear that."

He kissed her fingertips. "I'm glad you're not upset with me. Booze and drugs can make you do weird things. I'm free of them now. For today, at least. I've learned a hard lesson. It's truly one day at a time. That's not a cliché. It's a truism. No one knows what tomorrow will bring. All we can do is lay a good foundation today and work hard to make sure it doesn't crumble tomorrow."

Monica tilted her head. "How long have you been sober?"

"Three years and five months. But who's counting?" Daniel laughed. He reached into his pocket, and showed Monica his sobriety chip. "I always carry this with me."

Tears blurred Monica's vision. "That's so wonderful. I'm proud of you, Daniel. I can only imagine how hard this has been for you."

Nodding, Daniel agreed. "As I said, it's one day at a time. Those days would be a lot easier, if I had you by my side. I thought I was dreaming when I saw you leave the chapel tonight. I wanted to run to you, pick you up and swing you over my head. Lucky for you, I'm not still drinking." His grin lit his entire face. He reminded Monica of a little boy on Christmas morning.

Monica relaxed as she listened to Daniel. She sliced a piece of pie and then seductively wrapped her lips around the fork. A move she knew wouldn't be lost on Daniel.

His eyes hopeful, Daniel brightened. "You're still a little vixen, aren't you? My god, I've missed that."

"And I've missed you more than I thought possible." Her cheeks were on fire, as well as the rest of her body. "You're the only man who could bring me to such heights of ecstasy. I mean that. We were great together."

In a sensuous voice, Daniel whispered, "We'll be great together again, sweetheart, if you'll take me back."

"Perhaps we should table this discussion for now." Monica shifted in her seat and stroked his arms. She observed him for several moments before she found the courage to speak. "I think we should take this slow. Besides, it's late and I need to get home. Bandit will be wondering where I am."

"Bandit?"

"My dog. My loyal companion. She'll be wondering where her food is."

Daniel smiled. "She's a rescue dog, right? I know you. I'd bet my life you rescued her from somewhere or other. We can talk about us tomorrow. First thing in the morning? I doubt I'll get much sleep tonight."

Monica stood. "We'll talk in the morning. I promise."

Along with the money for the ticket, Daniel placed a generous tip on the table. The couple picked up their umbrellas and walked to the door together. Before they opened their umbrellas completely, the wind blew the rain through the opened door, dampening their clothing.

Daniel wrapped his free arm around Monica's waist. He leaned under the umbrella, and kissed her. "Won't you let me drive you home? We can leave your car. I can bring you back tomorrow to pick it up. That way, I'd know you're safe. I remember how you dislike driving in the rain."

Monica cupped Daniel's face in her hands. "Thanks for being so considerate, but I'll be fine. Call me about seven tomorrow morning? I don't think I'll get much sleep tonight either."

"How about instead of calling, I come straight to your house? I really want to meet Bandit." Daniel tugged his ear.

"I'm wise to you, Daniel Tanner." Monica laughed along with Daniel. "Bandit will want to meet you, too. I'll make breakfast for us. Do you still like scrambled eggs, bacon and potatoes?"

"Yes. I do. Some things never change."

Daniel gave Monica one last kiss. Together, they ran to her car. She wasted no time unlocking the door and flopping inside. Once she had blown Daniel a kiss, she started the car. In her rear view mirror, she saw Daniel watching her as she drove away, then he sprinted to his vehicle.

Monica couldn't wait until morning; she had to tell her sister everything. Though she refused to talk or text while she drove, she accelerated her speed. It took only seconds before the stupidity of her actions sank in. Reluctantly, she slowed her automobile to a more reasonable pace.

* * * *

As soon as Monica arrived home, she called Mandy. Mandy seemed excited. "So, what kind of flashy car does Daniel drive these days? Something big and expensive, I'll bet?"

Monica laughed. Her sister knew Daniel almost as well as she did. Probably because she'd shared everything with her. "No, he drives a Canary yellow sports car. It's probably worth more than I earn in a year. You too, for that matter, but then he gets such great deals from his uncle's dealership, so it doesn't matter. Can you believe he wanted to drive me home tonight because it's raining so hard? He said I'd be safer if he drove."

Mandy giggled. "I'm glad you didn't take him up on it. I still remember the night old lead foot gave me a ride home from your house. I swear; my muscles didn't unclench for a week. What if he had been drinking?" They both laughed as they remembered how scared Mandy was that night.

"He's coming over for breakfast tomorrow, and my stomach is doing flip-flops. I can't believe how nervous I am after all these years." Monica began to fidget. To calm herself, she took deep breaths. "This isn't going to be easy."

"Well, make sure you make something bland that you can hold down. Although, I'm not so sure throwing up on him is such a bad idea. He deserves some sort of punishment for casting you aside like yesterday's news."

A part of Monica agreed with Mandy, and she cringed at the thought of Daniel sitting in her kitchen covered with eggs and bacon. "As tempting as that is, girlfriend, I think maybe I should just serve cereal."

They chatted a bit longer. Monica couldn't believe that after twenty years, Daniel was a topic of their conversation. She thought he was permanently in the past. "I'll fill you in on everything once he's been here and gone."

"Hmm, I'm thinking that could be a long time, my friend," Mandy said, with a smile in her voice.

"Okay, don't put the cart before the horse, or I might throw up right now. Hey, it's time for Bandit's walk, so I'll talk to you later." Monica hung up and grabbed Bandit's leash. A walk might clear her head.

CHAPTER FIVE

Monica set her alarm for 5 a.m., but it wasn't necessary. She'd been up for a good half-hour before it buzzed. While she showered and shaved her legs, she hummed their song, *Wonderful Tonight*. Before *tonight* could happen, they'd need to have a long talk. Monica loved Daniel. That fact had never changed. She was certain he loved her, too. Yet, the possibility of becoming a couple again terrified her. Would they make the same mistakes? Would their love life be as exciting the second time around? Her main concern centered on his sobriety. Being alcohol or drug-free for three years didn't guarantee he wouldn't relapse; a reality she knew well. Addictions ran in her family. Several of her relatives suffered from the disease. Still, three plus years promised hope.

As Monica glanced at the clock on the wall, she quickened her stride. First, she prepared the coffee, and then set the table. When she looked at the clock again, it was ten minutes past seven. *"That's strange, Daniel is always punctual. At least, he used to be. It isn't raining, so the weather can't be a problem."*

Monica knew how much Daniel wanted to be with her. She thought for sure he'd arrive early. After giving Bandit her breakfast, she patted her faithful friend on the head. "We've got a visitor coming this morning, Bandit. I expect you to be on your best behavior. At least, I think we've got a visitor coming. It's 7:15, and still no Daniel. Do you think I should I call him, girl"?

The decision was taken out of her hands thirty minutes later by a knock on the door. Annoyed Daniel was so late, Monica waited a few seconds before she answered the door. *"At least, he was okay."* She didn't want to appear anxious.

"Who am I kidding? The breakfast is ruined. He'll know I'm aggravated and eager to give him a piece of my mind."

"So, you decided…" Monica said as she opened the door. Before her eyes focused, she realized it wasn't Daniel. "Mandy. What are you doing here so early? You usually don't get up until the crack of noon." She chuckled.

Mandy's eyes were wide. She didn't wait for Monica to open the door any further. Pushing her way inside, she placed her arms around her sister.

"Mandy. Mandy. What's up? Something's wrong. What is it?" Monica closed the door behind them. "Tell me. It's Daniel, isn't it?"

When Mandy spoke, she looked frightened. "So, you haven't heard from him? I took Mike to work this morning. His car broke down, and, and never mind about that. When we rounded the corner of Fifth and Mifflin, we saw Daniel's vehicle. I wouldn't have paid any attention, but the bright yellow sports car caught my eye."

Hands shaking, Monica sat down at the kitchen table, then pushed the dishes aside. "Tell me, Mandy. I can take it. Please, tell me."

As Mandy spoke, her voice cracked. "Monica, there was no ambulance, police car or anything. No one was in the car. Mike got out and checked. It appeared the accident happened much earlier. I think we should call the hospital. I'll call for you, if you can't."

Monica felt dizzy. Her ears buzzed, and she felt lightheaded. Her instincts had told her something was wrong. Why hadn't she listened to her inner voice? "Please, Mandy. Call Sea-Tac Hospital for me. I don't know whether I want him to be there, or not. I have no idea what could have happened."

In a beat, Mandy held the phone in her hand. She dialed the hospital. "Shh, Monica. I've got the hospital on the line. Yes. Daniel Tanner, please." Mandy inquired of the switchboard operator. After what seemed an eternity, Mandy said, "Okay. Thank you. Can you tell me his condition? No. Of course not. I understand. We'll be right there."

Mandy hung up the phone, and turned to Monica. "He's been admitted. The operator couldn't tell me anything else. Let's go. I'll drive."

If it was possible, Mandy drove even faster than old lead foot, Daniel. By the time they reached the hospital, a hundred different scenarios had played in Monica's head. *"Please, let him be alive, please."*

Dropping Monica at the front door, Mandy said, "You go inside. I'll park the car. Then, I'll meet you. And Monica, try not to worry. I'll be right with you."

* * * *

Inside the hospital, Monica waited for her sister at the reception desk. When Mandy hurried in, Monica grabbed her by the arm. Together, they walked to the elevators. "Daniel is on the third floor. Room 302. That's all they would tell me."

When the elevator doors opened, Monica forgot her good manners. She pushed her way inside, jostling the people who were on their way out. "Excuse us," Mandy pleaded on her behalf. A man in doctor's scrubs pushed the button for the third floor. As Monica prepared to ask the doctor about Daniel, the doors opened. The sisters rushed to the nurse's station.

Monica, her hands quivering and her voice shaking, spoke to the first nurse she saw. "Can you please tell me about Daniel Tanner? Is he alright? He's in room 302." She clutched the edge of the Formica counter so tightly that her fingers turned white.

"Are you related to the patient?" the charge nurse asked.

Again, Mandy spoke for her. Lying, she said "Monica is Daniel's sister."

The nurse signed something on her clipboard. "Very well. Dr. Robbins is in with a patient, but he'll be finished soon. He's the doctor in charge of your brother's case. He can fill you in on what happened. Oh, here he comes down the hall now."

Monica ran to Dr. Robbins. Breathless, she spoke. "Dr. Robbins, I'm Daniel Tanner's sister, Monica. Will you please tell me how he's doing? Is he going to be okay? How serious is his condition?"

Dr. Robbins gave Monica a practiced smile, and placed his hand on her shoulder. "He's okay as far as we've been able to determine. More tests will be required. He was in a single vehicle accident. Right now he has what we call, post-concussion syndrome, which involves headache and confusion."

Monica relaxed her shoulders, and breathed a big sigh. "So, there's nothing serious as far as you can tell? No broken bones or…"

The doctor escorted Monica to the nurse's station, a few feet away. "No, nothing is broken. Try not to worry. He's improved since he was admitted. We'll keep him overnight to run some standard tests. Since he was involved in a collision, we have to do a tox screen. I'm sure you're aware of the reason for the test."

In assent, Monica nodded her head. She was not one to pray, but she prayed for negative toxicology results. With Daniel's history, she knew it could go either way. "Yes. I understand, doctor. Is there anyone who can tell me what caused the accident?"

The physician explained as much as he knew about the accident. "According to the policeman, there was a witness to the accident. The officer told me a woman was walking her dog in the rainstorm. She saw the yellow car round the corner when a cat crossed the road. The driver swerved to avoid hitting the animal."

Monica's heart lightened for the first time since she'd heard about the accident. Mandy, who stood beside her, commented, "It doesn't surprise me that Daniel would do something like that. He has his faults, sis, but he wouldn't run over an animal if he could help it."

With a sigh of relief, Monica gave the doctor a hug. "Thank you so much. I feel better now, a whole lot better."

Doctor Robinson smiled at Monica. "After the tests, if everything checks out okay, he should be discharged tomorrow. You can look in on him now, but he won't know you're there. Why don't you come back later when you can have a proper visit?"

Monica relaxed the tension in her shoulders. "Thank you, Doctor," she said, as Dr. Robbins excused himself to attend another patient.

Looking at Monica, the nurse said, "You can't go in now. I'm afraid you'll have to wait here. Only two visitors at a time. His wife is already with him."

"Who?" Monica and Mandy exclaimed simultaneously. Monica felt the color drain from her face, and she thought she'd be sick. The tension returned to her shoulders. "I'm sorry. Did you say his wife?"

With a confused look, the young nurse replied, "Yes. That's what she said. I'm sure of it. Mr. Tanner is sleeping. He's been sedated since his arrival last night."

Trying to make sense of the puzzle, Monica thought for a moment. "Can you tell me if his wife has short red hair with a blonde streak on one side?"

The nurse didn't hesitate. "No, ma'am. She has blonde hair. Long, blonde hair. Nothing outstanding about her, really."

"Thank you, nurse." Monica grabbed her sister's elbow and led her away from the nurses' station. "Come on, Mandy. Let's get out of here. Now!" Monica whirled around, and then headed for the elevators.

"But, Monica," Mandy insisted. "You can't leave. You have to find out who this mysterious wife is. Don't you want to wait to see how Daniel is doing? What if something bad happens? This isn't like you. How can you *not* want to know?"

Exasperated, Monica sighed. "Mandy, you heard Dr. Robbins. He said Daniel will be fine." She jabbed the elevator button with her thumb again and again. "Come on, open!"

Finally, the elevator doors opened. Monica stormed inside. With unnecessary force, she pushed the button for the lobby. Seemingly at a loss for words, Mandy joined her.

"I don't need to find out who the mysterious woman is, Mandy. I'm certain whoever she is, she isn't his wife. I also know it isn't one of his sisters. The description doesn't match," Monica snapped. "I can't imagine who she might be. Probably, somebody he picked up after he said goodbye to me last night. Remember this—leopards never change their spots. I should've known this would happen. Well, it will never happen again. I don't want to talk about it anymore. Okay?"

Without offering the usual platitude of 'Everything will be okay,' Mandy hugged Monica. As the elevator descended to the lobby, they remained silent.

Likewise, during the ride to Monica's house, the sisters didn't say a word. When they arrived at Monica's place, she broke the silence. "Thanks for always being here for me.

You always understand. I'll call you tomorrow. Right now, I really need to be alone."

Monica gave her sister a quick hug and then got out of the car. She strolled along the brick walkway to her house and watched Mandy drive away.

Bandit greeted her in her usual effusive fashion. "Come on, Bandit," Monica said, scratching behind the dog's ear. "Let's go to the park for a run." Excited, Bandit ran around in circles. She knew the word *park* and she loved running with the other dogs. "I could use a good run myself. I have a lot of anger to get out of my system." She slipped into her running gear, fastened Bandit's leash to her collar, and off they went.

* * * *

When Monica returned home, she checked her voice mail. There were no messages. She wasn't expecting any, but still...

Monica fed Bandit, and then turned on her computer. Did she hope to concentrate on work? Fortunately, the operative reports were easy. She surprised herself by getting through the morning's batch.

After eating a light lunch and taking Bandit for another walk, Monica went back to work. At 4:30, the loud ring of the phone startled her. It was Mandy. "Hey, Monica. Any news about Daniel? Before you bite my head off, I know you said you don't care, but..."

"It's okay, Mandy. I'm much calmer now. When the phone rang, I thought it might be Daniel. I'm going to call the hospital when we hang up. It's killing me not knowing what's going on. I know that'll make you feel better."

Mandy blew a low whistle into the phone. "I'll admit I'm glad you're checking on Daniel. I won't keep you. Call me after you find out how he's doing, okay?"

Monica placed the phone back on the receiver, and paced the kitchen floor. She tried to summon the courage to call the hospital. For the second time, the phone rang, jangling her nerves. She took a deep breath. "Hello."

A sleepy voice whispered, "Hello, sweetheart. It's me. But then again who else would it be?" Daniel's remark was met with silence. "Monica?"

In an even tone, Monica answered, "I'm happy to know you're awake, Daniel. Are you feeling well?"

Daniel's voice was urgent now. "What's up? You sound so distant. Did I do something? I mean something other than wrap my car around a pole? I need to see you — tell you what happened, and why I didn't show up this morning."

Resisting the urge to scream, Monica paced again. "I know enough. I don't need to know anything else, Daniel. I'm glad to hear you're fine. Mandy and I were at the hospital early this morning. Dr. Robbins assured us you would recover."

"So you left without seeing me? Why?" Monica heard the anguish in Daniel's voice, but she refused to fall for his tricks.

"We figured you had enough company. I'm sure your wife wouldn't have wanted us to intrude."

"Did you say my wife?" Daniel's voice escalated. He no longer sounded sleepy.

"Yes. You heard right. Your wife. The nurse told me your wife was in the room with you. Look, I doubt that the woman was your wife. Don't bother denying it. There was a woman in your room, and that's enough for me. I don't need a repeat of twenty years ago. And by the way, I also know it wasn't either of your sisters. Forget you walked back into my life. Goodbye."

As soon as she hung up the phone, it rang. Seething, Monica didn't bother to answer. For the next hour, it rang repeatedly. Finally, it stopped. Monica made a pot of coffee. She wouldn't get much sleep tonight anyway.

TOO YOUNG TO BE THIS OLD

CHAPTER SIX

The next morning, Monica awakened to an insistent pounding on her front door. It had to be Daniel. With a gentle, but firm hand, she scooted Bandit off the bed. "Okay, girl. We might as well get this over and done with. I'll let you out in the backyard, while I take care of this."

After throwing on a pair of jeans and a tee shirt, Monica let Bandit out the back door. "I'm coming," she yelled, as she walked to the front door and opened it. Before she had a chance to speak, Daniel threw his arms around her and held her tight. "Daniel," she screamed, "let me go! You're squeezing the breath out of me."

Daniel released Monica, and took a step backwards. He gazed into Monica's eyes. "I need to talk to you, but first, please let me sweeten the deal." He pulled her near, and kissed her. Stroking her back, he allowed his hand to roam from her spine to her hair. Next, he sifted her silky tresses with his fingers. When she tried to pull away, he hugged her tighter. "No matter what you think is going on, Monica, it isn't. I don't have a wife. I don't have a girlfriend. I don't even have a lover. You're the only woman for me, now and forever. Will you please let me in? It's cold out here. Please."

Monica stepped back and allowed Daniel to enter the house. "You can come in for a minute, she muttered, rolling her eyes at him, "but only because I don't want you to catch a cold and end up in the hospital again."

Daniel cast his gaze about the room. "May I sit somewhere? After all, I just got discharged from the hospital, remember?"

Monica led Daniel into the living room. "Have a seat, Daniel." She pointed to the couch. Once he sat, she occupied the space at the opposite end of the sofa. Her emotions were twisted in a knot. Although she wanted to slap him silly, she also had an overpowering desire to ravish him "Not that I'll believe you, but who was the woman in the room with you?"

Daniel smiled. "You mean my wife?" Monica gasped and stood, ready to show him the door. Still grinning, Daniel exclaimed, "Hold on, Monica." He grabbed both her hands and pulled her back to the sofa. "I omitted an important prefix, just as the nurse did at the hospital. Ex."

"X? X what?"

"Ex, as in my ex-wife, sweetheart. Or as you like to point out, my *first* ex-wife. Rachel was in the room with me. Not that I could vouch for that. I was pretty much out of it at the time. She called later to check on me. That's when I discovered she'd come to see me."

"How did she know you were in the hospital? Or, was she in the car with you?" Monica tugged against Daniel's grasp, but he wouldn't let go.

"The hospital called her. When they went through my belongings, they found my cell phone. Her name's listed as an ICE, In Case of Emergency. I told you we're very good friends. I feel closer to her than either of my sisters. That's why her name was listed as the emergency contact. Had the accident happened later, your number would've been listed. We'd just gotten back together. At least, I hope we're back together."

Monica heard a mixture of the anguish, sadness, and hope in his voice.

"I didn't have time to program your number. Everything I've just told you is the truth. You have to believe me."

As they sat on the couch, Daniel told her about the accident. When he spoke of avoiding the cat, he winked. That confession brought a smile to Monica's face. "Not only are you a sentimental man, but you're a kind man. The world needs more people like you. I'm so happy you're still in it."

Daniel gazed at Monica. "I'll always put my life on the line for you. No alcohol or pills could ever make me feel as happy as you do. You're my drug of choice. This is one wagon I don't ever want to fall off, my precious,

Monica." He brushed his knee against hers, while caressing her leg. "Just give me one last chance. That's all I'll need. I promise I'll never screw up again. It was a long, hard lesson to learn. I love you. I always have, and I always will. I've carried this torch for you for over twenty years. I know together we can keep it lit for fifty more."

"I love you, Daniel. I've carried a torch for you, too." She placed her right hand to her heart. "You stole this heart twenty years ago. I wanted it back, but not anymore. It's yours to keep. Forever."

How bittersweet that it took a funeral to awaken them to life, and love. Sometimes, life gives us a second chance. Only the prideful will pass it by.

~THE END~

About the Author

Sheryl Letzgus McGinnis

Born in Queensland, Australia, Sheryl McGinnis is a proud Australian-American. She has authored four drug addiction books, and numerous other publications. A former radio disk jockey and television voice-over artist, Sheryl uses her talents to keep kids off drugs. Jack McGinnis is her husband, and she's a mother as well. Animals are also her passion; Sheryl is the Founder of a humane society in North Carolina.

To learn more about Sheryl Letzgus McGinnis, visit her website: www.sherylletzgusmcginnis.com

E-mail:sherrymcg@cfl.rr.com

http://www.topazpublishingllc.com

www.ingramcontent.com/pod-product-compliance
Lightning Source LLC
Chambersburg PA
CBHW060509030426
42337CB00015B/1807

* 9 7 8 0 6 1 5 9 3 0 2 7 5 *